KU-503-211

CONTENTS

INTRODUCTION

Holiday Greek is a short course which will equip you to deal with everyday situations when you visit Greece and Cyprus: shopping, eating out, asking for directions, changing money (a different currency is used in Cyprus), using the phones and so on.

The course is divided into seven main sections, covering 22 situations corresponding to the everyday activities of two characters on holiday in Greece: Anne Johnson on her first visit to Athens, and Peter Hunt on his second trip to Paros in the Aegean. Each unit begins with a dialogue, which introduces the essential language items in context. Key phrases are highlighted in the dialogues, and the phrasebook section which follows lists these and other useful phrases and tells you what they are in English.

Within the units there are also short information sections in English on the topics covered, sections giving basic grammatical explanation, and a number of follow-up activities designed to be useful as well as fun. Answers can be checked in a key at the back of the book.

BEFORE YOU LEAVE

Introduction to modern Greek

Holiday Greek offers a starter course in modern Greek, and does not attempt to cover Greek grammar comprehensively or in detail. This introduction is to help you understand a few basics about modern Greek grammar. The units that follow will explain everything again, but if you read this first, you'll be better prepared.

Greek nouns, adjectives and articles ('a' and 'the' in English) change their endings according to gender, number and function in the sentence.

Gender Greek nouns (names of people and things) are divided into three groups: masculine, feminine, neuter. To recognise the gender of the noun, learn the form of the article that goes with it. All nouns in this book will be listed with this article. Some examples:

ο πατέρας *o pateras* (the father) – masculine
η μητέρα *i mitera* (the mother) – feminine
το παιδί *to pethi* (the child) – neuter

One you have learnt the typical endings of these three genders, you can guess the gender of any Greek word. French is not so easy!

Number Nouns, and adjectives that qualify them, have two forms: singular for one item: plural for more than one. (see page 13).

Hara Garoufalia

Series editors: Shirley Baldwin and Sarah Boas

Hodder & Stoughton

A MEMBER OF THE HODDER HEADLINE GROUP

ACKNOWLEDGEMENTS

The author and publisher would like to thank J. Allan Cash for the
photograph on page 10, and Barnaby's Picture Library for the
photograph on page 85. All other photographs are reproduced by
kind permission of Howard Middle.

Long-renowned as the authoritative source for self-guided
learning – with more than 30 million copies sold worldwide –
the *Teach Yourself* series includes over 200 titles in the fields
of languages, crafts, hobbies, sports, and other leisure activities.

British Library Cataloguing in Publication Data
Garoufalia-Middle, Hara
    Holiday Greek
    I. Title
    489.383421
ISBN 0 340 63124 4

First published 1988 as *Greek in a week*
Re-published 1995 as *Teach Yourself Holiday Greek*
Impression number   10   9   8   7   6   5   4   3   2   1
Year   1999 1998 1997 1996 1995

Copyright © 1988; 1995 Hara Garoufalia

Typeset by Transet Ltd, Coventry, Warwickshire.
Printed in Great Britain by Butler & Tanner Ltd, Frome and London, for
Hodder & Stoughton Educational, a division of Hodder Headline Plc,
338 Euston Road, London NW1 3BH.

INTRODUCTION

Function in the sentence   Greek nouns have three forms, called cases, indicating: the subject (nominative case); the object (accusative case); possession (genitive case).

The nominative case is used to show the subject of the sentence – the person or thing carrying out an action:

Ο πατέρας θέλει ένα καφέ   *o pateras thelei ena kafe*   The father wants a coffee

Here, the father is the subject. The article is 'ο', in the nominative case for a masculine noun. Nominative is also used for the subject of the verb **είμαι** *ime* (to be).

The accusative case is used to show the object of the sentence – the person or thing to which the action is done, e.g.:

Η Μαρία αγαπάει τον πατέρα   *I Maria agapai ton patera*   Maria loves the father

Notice how the nominative 'ο' changes to the accusative 'τον' *ton*.

The accusative case always follows prepositions (words of place or direction), e.g.:

απο την Κρήτη	*apo tin Kriti*	from Crete
για τη Ρόδο	*ya ti Rotho*	for Rhodes
στην Αθήνα	*stin Athina*	in/to Athens

The genitive case is used to show who or what owns something, e.g.:

Το σπίτι του Γιώργου	*to spiti too Yiorgoo*	George's house
Το βιβλίο της Μαρίας	*to vivlio tis Marias*	Maria's book

Articles   In Greek the definite article ('the' in English) and the indefinite article ('a' in English) change according to the number, gender and case of the nouns they define (see Monday, page 12).

Word order   Because of the changes to words mentioned above, you can perceive in Greek more clearly the function of words in a sentence. In English you have to rely on word order to tell you who is doing what to whom – compare 'Peter loves Anne' with 'Anne loves Peter'. In Greek, word order is more flexible, as you will discover.

Verbs   In Greek, verbs ('doing' words) have endings which change according to the subject, the person or thing doing the action. In English we have to put 'I', 'you', 'we', etc., in front of the verb. In Greek **κάνω**/*kano* means 'I make'. **κάνεις**/*kaneis* means 'you make'. The ending is sufficient to show the subject. Of course, Greeks have words for 'I', 'you', etc., but these are used more for emphasis.

'You' forms   Like French, but not like English, Greek has two forms for 'you': a 'familiar' form for friends, children, relatives; a polite form used for people you don't know, particularly older people or those in authority. This polite form is also the plural of 'you', which you'd use for more than one friend or relative.

The familiar form is **εσύ**/*esi*. The polite/plural form is **εσείς**/*esis*.

INTRODUCTION

The Greek Alphabet

The Greek alphabet has twenty-four letters: seven vowels and seventeen consonants.

Letter		Name	Sound
A	α	alfa	like a in rather
B	β	vita	like v in vet
Γ	γ	ghama	before a, o, u sounds, g made at the back of the throat; before e and i, like y in yet
Δ	δ	thelta	like th in that
E	ε	epsilon	like e in envy
Z	ζ	zita	like z in zebra
H	η	ita	like i in ill
Θ	θ	thita	like th in theatre
I	ι	iota	before a and o, like y in yet; otherwise like i in ill
K	κ	kapa	like k in key
Λ	λ	lambda	like l in law
M	μ	mi	like m in match
N	ν	ni	like n in nut
Ξ	ξ	ksi	like x in mix
O	o	omikron	like o in olive
Π	π	pi	like p in pet
P	ρ	ro	like r in red
Σ	σ, ς	sighma	like s in soft
T	τ	taf	like t in top
Υ	υ	ipsilon	like i in ill
Φ	φ	fi	like f in fire
X	χ	khi	before e or i, like h in hand; otherwise like ch in loch (Scottish lake)
Ψ	ψ	psi	like ps in collapse
Ω	ω	omegha	like o in olive

INTRODUCTION

You will notice that **η** ita, **ι** iota, and **υ** ipsilon, are all pronounced the same. Likewise **o** omikron and **ω** omegha.

You will also notice that **θ** and **δ** are spelt the same in transliteration, but are pronounced differently. In order to aid pronunciation, you will find that where th is derived from **δ** it remains in italic *-th-* (all transliterations in this book are italicised) and where it is derived from **θ** it is in the normal text face -th.

ς sigma is used only at the end of words.

Note: only one syllable is normally stressed in a Greek word. This is marked with an acute ´ accent.

Some extra notes on pronunciation

Double vowels (diphthongs)   A diphthong consists of two vowels which are pronounced together to make only one sound.

αι   is like e in hen, e.g. **αίμα**/*ema* (blood)
οι   is like ee in meet (but kept short), e.g. **οικογένεια**/*ikoyenia* (family)
ει   is also like ee in meet, e.g. **είσοδος**/*eesothos* (entrance)
αυ   is either af as in **αυτοκίνητο**/*aftokinito* (car), or
         av as in **αυγό**/*avgo* (egg)
ευ   is either eff as in **ευχαριστώ**/*efharisto* (thank you), or
         ev as in **Ευρώπη**/*evropi* (Europe)
ου   is like oo as in boot, e.g. **μπουζούκι**/*boozooki*

Combinations of consonants

μπ   at the beginning of a word is like b in bed: **μπάρ**/*bar* (bar)
μπ   in the middle of a word is like mb as **γάμπα**/*ghamba* (leg)
ντ   at the beginning of a word is like d in door **ντους**/*doosh* (shower)
ντ   in the middle of a word is like nd as in end **έντεκα**/*endeka* (11)
γκ   at the beginning of a word is like g in get **γκάζι**/*gazi* (gas)
γκ   in the middle of a word is like ng as in sting **αγκίστρι**/*angistri* (hook)
γγ   is like ng in song, e.g. **Άγγλος**/*anglos* (only in the middle of a word)
τσ   is like ts as in bits, e.g. **τσιγάρο**/*tsigaro* (cigarette)
τζ   is like tz as in jazz, e.g. **τζατζίκι**/*tzatziki* (yoghurt and garlic dip)

Note: double consonants are pronounced as if they were single, e.g. **θάλασσα**/th*alassa* (sea).

1 ARRIVALS AND GREETINGS

ARRIVING IN GREECE

Hotels are given ratings: Luxury, A, B, C (or Γ ghama in Greek). B and C rated hotels will have a breakfast room, but probably not a restaurant. Resort hotels may offer full or more usually half board.

A hotel guide is available from the Greek National Tourist Office.

Καλημέρα/Good morning

Anne Johnson is a bank clerk, on her first visit to Athens. She has always been interested in Ancient Greece, and has been studying Greek at evening classes.

Anne has now arrived at Athens International Airport, has collected her luggage, gone through customs, and is now looking for a taxi to her hotel.

Anne: **Καλημέρα.**
kalimera.
Taxi driver: Καλημέρα σας.
kalimera sas.
Anne: Ξενοδοχείο Ακρόπολη
ksenothoheeo akropoli
παρακαλώ.
parakalo.
Taxi driver: Μάλιστα κυρία.
malista, kiria.
Anne: Εδώ είναι η βαλίτσα μου.
etho ine i valitsa moo.
Ευχαριστώ.
efharisto.

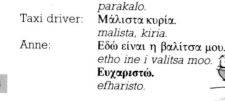

1 ARRIVALS AND GREETINGS

Words and phrases from the dialogue

Καλημέρα	kalimera	good morning
Ξενοδοχείο	ksenothoheeo	hotel
Παρακαλώ	parakalo	please/you're welcome/can I help?*
Μάλιστα	malista	of course/certainly
Κυρία	kiria	madam/Mrs
Ευχαριστώ	efharisto	thank you
Εδώ είναι	etho ine	here is
η βαλίτσα μου	i valitsa moo	my suitcase

* Παρακαλώ/parakalo means: 'please' in a request
'you're welcome' after 'thank you'
'can I help you?' in a shop

Other useful phrases

Καλησπέρα	kalispera	good evening
Καληνύχτα	kalinihta	good night
Χαίρετε	herete	hello/goodbye (formal)*
Γειά σου/σας	ya soo/sas	hello/goodbye (informal)
Κύριος	kirios	Mr
Δεσποινίς	thespinis	Miss
Τι κάνεις/κάνετε;	ti kanis/kanete?	How are you?
Καταλαβαίνω	katalaveno	I understand
Δεν καταλαβαίνω	then katalaveno	I don't understand
Μιλάτε Αγγλικά;	milate anglika?	Do you speak English?

* Γειά σου/ya soo is used with one person you know well;
Γειά σας/ya sas is used with more than one person, or with one person you don't know.

How to address people in Greek

Mr Κύριος/kírios (note the stress on the first syllable)
Mrs Κυρία/kiría (second syllable stressed)
Miss Δεσποινίς/thespinís

Greeks don't yet have a word for 'Ms' – when in doubt use κυρία/kiria.

When you call to someone male, e.g. a waiter, κύριος/kírios changes its ending to κύριε/kirie.

Yes and No

Be careful! 'Yes' in Greek – Ναι/ne – sounds a bit like 'no'.

'No' is Όχι/ohi. Greeks will often indicate 'no' with a combination of raising their eyebrows and making a 'tut' sound.

One of the most useful words in Greek is Εντάξει/endaksi – OK.

1 ACCOMMODATION

FINDING ACCOMMODATION

Pensions   Alternatives to hotels, especially on the islands, are 'pensions' **Πανσιόν**/*pansion*, or private houses, where rooms (**Δωμάτια**/*thomatia*) can be rented for short periods. There are usually agencies on the harbour front where rooms can be booked, and people touting for business as each boat comes in. Look out for the sign:

ΝΟΙΚΙΑΖΟΥΜΕ ΔΩΜΑΤΙΑ   or just   ΔΩΜΑΤΙΑ

Campsites are plentiful, and are often advertised by roadside signs miles before their location. Olympia for example has many sites, some with shops, swimming pool and other facilities. A Camping Guide is obtainable from the Greek National Tourist Office (EOT).

Please note   Greek authorities do not allow tourists to sleep on beaches. You will, on arrival, be expected to have some proof of accommodation arrangements.

1 ACCOMMODATION

θέλω ενα δωμάτιο, παρακαλώ
I want a room, please

Peter Hunt is a sales representative, on his second trip to the Greek islands. He's crazy about all kinds of water sports, and night life!

Peter has just got off the boat from Piraeus, and is now looking for somewhere to stay on the beautiful island of Paros. He hasn't bothered to book in advance. Typical!

Travel agent:	Δωμάτια, δωμάτια! Rooms, rooms!
	thomatia, thomatia! Rooms, rooms!
Peter:	**Θέλω ένα δωμάτιο, παρακαλώ.**
	thelo ena thomatio, parakalo.
Travel agent:	Για πόσες μέρες;
	ya posses meres?
Peter:	Για πέντε μέρες. Έχετε;
	ya pende meres. Ehete?
Travel agent:	Ναι, βεβαίως, κύριε. Έχω ένα πολύ ωραίο, κοντά στη
	ne, veveos, kirie. Eho ena poli oreo, konda sti
	θάλασσα.
	thalassa.
Peter:	**Πόσο κάνει;**
	posso kanee?
Travel agent:	Το δωμάτιο είναι πολύ φτηνό. Μόνο δύο χιλιάδες
	to thomatio ine poli ftino. mono thio hiliathes
	δραχμές με ντους.
	thrakmes, me doosh.
Peter:	Εντάξει. Ευχαριστώ.
	endaksi. efharisto.

1 ACCOMMODATION

Words and phrases from the dialogue

Θέλω ένα δωμάτιο	thelo ena thomatio	I want a room
Για πόσες μέρες;	ya posses meres?	for how many days?
Για πέντε μέρες	ya pende meres	for five days
Έχετε;	ehete?	Do you have (any)?
Βεβαίως	veveos	of course
Έχω ένα πολύ ωραίο	eho ena poli oreo	I have a very nice one
Κοντά στη θάλασσα	konda sti thalassa	near the sea
Πόσο κάνει;	posso kani?	How much?
Πολύ φτηνό	poli ftino	very cheap
Μόνο δύο χιλιάδες δραχμές	mono thio hiliathes thrakmes	only 2000 drachmas
Με ντους	me doosh	with a shower

Other useful phrases

Σήμερα	simera	today
Χθες	hthes	yesterday
Αύριο	avrio	tomorrow
(η) μέρα	(i) mera	day
(η) νύχτα	(i) nihta	night (after midnight)
(το) πρωί	(to) proee	early morning
(το) βράδυ	(to) vrathee	evening (7.00 to 12.00 pm)
(το) απόγευμα	(to) apoyevma	afternoon (3.00 to 7.00 pm)
(το) μεσημέρι	(to) mesimeri	noon (between 12 noon and 3)

The siesta Especially in the hot summer months, Greek people have several hours of rest after lunch – between 2.00 pm and 5.30 pm – before going back to work for the evening period. People try not to make too much noise, or play their stereos loud during this time. After 5.30, though, life gets going again.

the way it works

Definite article

You saw in the dialogue the word for 'the' **το**/*to*, used with the word **δωμάτιο**/*thomatio* (room). **Δωμάτιο**/*thomatio* is a neuter noun.

With a feminine noun, e.g. **βαλίτσα**/*valitsa* (suitcase), the definite article form is **η** (*i*), as in **η βαλίτσα**.

With a masculine noun, the article is **ο** (*o*), e.g. **ο όροφος**/*o orofos* (floor of a house/hotel) – see the dialogue on page 14.

Indefinite article

The equivalent forms for the indefinite article ('a' in English) are:

1 ACCOMMODATION

masculine:	ἕνας	enas	ἕνας κύριος	enas kirios	a man
feminine:	μία	mia	μία κυρία	mia kiria	a lady
neuter:	ἕνα	ena	ἕνα παιδί	ena pethi	a child

These are the nominative forms (see Introduction) – you'll see later how these forms change according to the function (case) of the noun in the sentence.

Plural   Note that δωμάτιο/*thomatio* becomes δωμάτια/*thomatia* in the plural. Η μέρα/*I mera* (the day) becomes μέρες/*meres*, in Για πόσες μέρες/*ya posses meres*. These are typical ways neuter and feminine nouns change in the plural (see page 33 for a full list of plural forms).

Note: In this book all nouns listed are given in the nominative case, i.e. the case used with the subject of the sentence.

Possessive adjectives

Note that the definite article comes *before* the noun, and the possessive adjective comes *after*.

The Greek word for 'my' (possessive adjective) is μου/*moo*.

Η βαλίτσα μου   *i valitsa moo*   my suitcase

Unlike French or German, where the 'my' form changes with gender and number, in Greek the form is constant – a lot easier!

The possessive adjectives are:

μου	*moo*	my	μας	*mas*	our
σου	*soo*	your (sing./fam.)	σας	*sas*	your (pl./polite)
του	*too*	his	τους	*toos*	their (masc.)
της	*tis*	her	τους	*toos*	their (fem.)
του	*too*	its	τους	*toos*	their (neut.)

e.g.:

Το δωμάτιό σας είναι το εκατόν είκοσι   your room is number 120
to thomatio sas ine to ekaton ikosi

Το διαβατήριό μου είναι εδώ   my passport is here
to thiavatirio moo ine etho

Το τσάϊ μας είναι κρύο   our tea is cold
to tsai mas ine krio

things to do

.1   Practise greeting the following people, at different times of the day:

1   Mrs Pavlou, hotel manager (say good morning)
2   Mr Stavropoulos, a business contact (say good evening)
3   Maria, a friend (say a friendly hello)
4   Miss Niarchou (say a formal hello)

1 ACCOMMODATION

AT THE HOTEL

Ένα μονόκλινο, με μπάνιο
A single room with bath

Anne Johnson arrives at her hotel, where, unlike Peter, she has booked in advance. The Hotel Acropolis is a pleasant B category hotel not far from the Plaka.

Hotel clerk: **Παρακαλώ;**
parakalo?

Anne: **Το όνομά μου είναι** Johnson. **Ορίστε το διαβατήριό μου.**
to onoma mou ine Johnson. oriste to thiavatirio mou.

Clerk: **Α! ναι, κυρία** Johnson. **Το δωμάτιό σας είναι έτοιμο.**
ah, ne, Kiria Johnson. to thromatio sas ine etimo.
Ένα μονόκλινο με μπάνιο.
Ena monoklino, me banyo.

Anne: **Πολύ καλά, ευχαριστώ. Τι όροφος, παρακαλώ;**
poli kala, efharisto. ti orofos, parakalo?

Clerk: **Το δωμάτιό σας είναι το εκατόν είκοσι, στον πρώτο όροφο.**
to thomatio sas ine to ekaton ikosi, ston proto orofo.

Anne: **Εντάξει. Τι ώρα έχει πρωϊνό;**
endaksi. ti ora ehi proino?

Clerk: **Από τις επτά, μέχρι τις δέκα. Εδώ είναι το κλειδί σας.**
apo tis epta, mehri tis theka. Etho ine to kleethi sas.
Καλώς ωρίσατε!
kalos orisate!

Words and phrases from the dialogue

Το όνομά μου είναι	*to onoma mou ine*	my name is …
Ορίστε	*oriste*	here it is
Το διαβατήριό μου	*to thiavatirio moo*	my passport
Το δωμάτιό σας είναι έτοιμο	*to thomatio sas ine etimo*	your room is ready
Ένα μονόκλινο με μπάνιο	*ena monoklino, me banyo*	a single, with bath

1 ACCOMMODATION

Πολύ καλά	poli kala	very good/fine
Τι όροφος;	ti orofos?	Which floor?
Το εκατόν είκοσι	to ekaton ikosi	number 120
στον πρώτο όροφο	ston proto orofo	on the first floor
Τι ώρα;	ti ora ...?	What time ...?
Το πρωϊνό	to proino	breakfast
Απο τις ... μέχρι τις ...	apo tis ... mehri tis ...	from ... to ...
Το κλειδί σας	to kleethi sas	your key
Καλώς ωρίσατε!	kalos orisate!	Welcome!

Numbers 0–22

0	μηδέν	mithen	11	ένδεκα	entheka
1	ένα/μία/ένας	ena/mia/enas	12	δώδεκα	thotheka
2	δυο	thio	13	δεκατρία	thekatria
3	τρία/τρείς	tria/tris	14	δεκατέσσερα	thekatessera
4	τέσσερα	tessera	15	δεκαπέντε	thekapende
	τέσσερις	tesseris	16	δεκαέξη	thekaeksi
5	πέντε	pende	17	δεκαεπτά	theka-epta
6	έξι	eksi	18	δεκαοκτώ	theka-okto
7	εφτά/επτά	efta/epta	19	δεκαεννέα	theka-enea
8	οκτώ/οχτώ	okto/ohto	20	είκοσι	ikosi
9	εννέα/εννιά	enea/ennia	21	είκοσι ένα	ikosi ena
10	δέκα	theka	22	είκοσι δύο	ikosi thio

	Greek	Translit		Greek	Translit
1st	πρώτος	protos	7th	έβδομος	evthomos
2nd	δεύτερος	thefteros	8th	όγδοος	ogthoos
3rd	τρίτος	tritos	9th	ένατος	enatos
4th	τέταρτος	tetartos	10th	δέκατος	thekatos
5th	πέμπτος	pemptos	11th	ενδέκατος	enthekatos
6th	έκτος	ektos			

Other useful phrases

Έχω κλείσει	eho kleesee	I've booked
Έχετε δωμάτια	ehete thomatia	Do you have any rooms?
Μπορώ να το δω;	boro na to tho?	Can I see it?
(Ένα) μονόκλινο	(ena) monoklino	a single room
(Ένα) δίκλινο	(ena) diklino	a double room
(Ένα) τρίκλινο	(ena) triklino	a 3-bed room
Με διπλό κρεβάτι	me thiplo krevati	with a double bed
Με δύο κρεβάτια	me thio krevatya	with two beds
Υπογράψτε	ipograpste	sign (please)
Δεν έχουμε	then ehoume	We don't have (any)
Είμαστε γεμάτοι	imaste yemati	We're full
Η τουαλέττα	i tooaleta	toilet
Η πετσέτα	i petseta	towel
Το σαπούνι	to sapooni	soap
Το χαρτί τουαλέττας	to harti tooaletas	toilet paper
Ο λογαριασμός	o logariasmos	bill

1 ACCOMMODATION

the way it works

Neuter nouns

Neuter nouns can be recognised by their endings *o, ι -μα*, e.g.:

το δωμάτιο	*to thomatio*	the room
το διαβατήριο	*to thiavatirio*	the passport
το κλειδί	*to kleethi*	the key
το όνομα	*to onoma*	the name

(see page 33 for masculine and feminine forms)

Adjectives

Adjectives in Greek have to agree with the noun they qualify, e.g.:

Το δωμάτιο είναι έτοιμο *to thomatio ine etimo* the room is ready

Verbs

You have met three important verbs so far:

Θέλω the*lo* I want   **έχω** *eho* I have   **είμαι** *ime* I am

When you talk about a verb in Greek you use the 'I' form, as there is no infinitive (to have).

This is how a regular Greek verb is conjugated:

Θέλω	the*lo*	I want	**Θέλουμε**	the*loome*	we want
Θέλεις	the*lis*	you want (sing.)	**Θέλετε**	the*lete*	you want (plur.)
Θέλει	the*li*	he/she/it wants	**Θέλουν(ε)**	the*loon(e)*	they want

eho (I have) has the same endings:

Έχω	*eho*	I have	**Έχουμε**	*ehoome*	we have
Έχεις	*ehis*	you have	**Έχετε**	*ehete*	you have
Έχει	*ehi*	he/she/it has	**Έχουν(ε)**	*ehoon(e)*	they have

However, *ime* (I am) is irregular:

Είμαι	*ime*	I am	**Είμαστε**	*imaste*	we are
Είσαι	*ise*	you are (sing.)	**Είστε/είσαστε**	*iste/isaste*	you are (plur.)
Είναι	*ine*	he/she/it is	**Είναι**	*ine*	they are

Note: The polite form of 'you': you normally use the second person *plural* form of the verb when talking to someone you don't know well.

Negative/Interrogative

The negative is easy in Greek – just put, δεν pronounced 'then' in front of the verb:

Δεν έχουμε δωμάτια/*then ehoome thomatia* – we don't have any rooms.

To ask a question only the intonation changes, not the word order, as in English. Listen again, if you have the cassette.

ORDERING BREAKFAST

Personal pronouns

In the Introduction we noted that Greeks do not use personal pronouns as much as in English, because the endings of the verbs themselves give the person. Greek personal pronouns are:

Εγώ	*ego*	I	**Εμείς**	*emis*	we
Εσύ	*esi*	you (sing. fam. form)	**Εσείς**	*esis*	you (plural, formal)
Αυτός	*aftos*	he	**Αυτοί**	*afti*	they (m.)
Αυτή	*afti*	she	**Αυτές**	*aftes*	they (f.)
Αυτό	*afto*	it	**Αυτά**	*afta*	they (n.)

Τσάϊ με λεμόνι, παρακαλώ
Tea with lemon, please

In the hotel restaurant, Anne decides to have a late breakfast.

Waiter: Καλημέρα κυρία. Τσάϊ ή καφέ;
            Kalimera kiria. tsai i kafe?

Anne: **Τσάϊ με λεμόνι παρακαλώ.**
            tsai me lemoni parakalo.

Waiter: Θέλετε αυγά με μπέϊκον;
            thelete avga me beicon?

Anne: **Όχι ευχαριστώ.** Μόνο τόστ, βούτυρο και μαρμελάδα.
            ohi efharisto. mono tost, vootiro ke marmelatha.

Waiter: Μάλιστα. **Ο αριθμός του δωματίου σας;**
            malista. o arithmos too thomatioo sas?

Anne: Εκατόν είκοσι.
            ekaton ikosi.

Words and phrases from the dialogue

τσάϊ ή καφέ	tsai i kafe	tea or coffee
με λεμόνι	me lemoni	with lemon
αυγά με μπέϊκον	avga me beicon	eggs and bacon
μόνο τόστ	mono tost	only toast
το βούτυρο	to vootiro	butter
η μαρμελάδα	i marmelatha	jam/marmalade
ο αριθμός	o arithmos	number
του δωματίου σας	too thomatioo sas	of your room
εκατόν είκοσι	ekaton ikosi	120

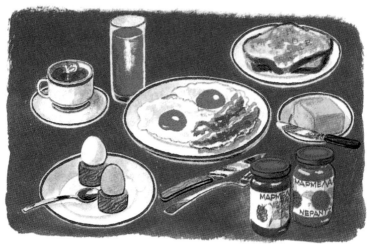

Other useful phrases

το πρωϊνό	to proino	breakfast
το μεσημεριανό	to mesimeriano	lunch
το βραδινό	to vrathino	dinner
το γάλα	to gala	milk
χυμός πορτοκάλι	himos portokali	orange juice
καφές με γάλα	kafes me gala	coffee with milk
χωρίς γάλα	horis gala	without milk
ακόμα λίγο καφέ,	akoma ligo kafe,	more coffee,
παρακαλώ	parakalo	please
το αλάτι	to alati	salt
το πιπέρι	to piperi	pepper
ζεστό νερό	zesto nero	hot water
βραστό αυγό	vrasto avgo	boiled egg
τηγανητό αυγό	tiganito avgo	fried egg
η ζάχαρη	i zahari	sugar
το ψωμί	to psomi	bread
το μαχαίρι	to maheri	knife
το πηρούνι	to pirooni	fork
το κουτάλι	to kootali	spoon

1   ACCOMMODATION

things to do

1.2 Practise booking different sorts of room at an hotel. Use **θέλω** the*lo* (I want/I would like).

1

2

3

4

5

1.3 You have arrived at a hotel where you have a reservation. Can you fill in your part of the conversation with the receptionist?

You:	(say good morning)
Receptionist:	Το όνομά σας, παρακαλώ;
	to onoma sas, parakalo?
You:	(give your name)
Receptionist:	Ναι, ένα δίκλινο, με ντους. Το διαβατήριό σας;
	ne, ena thiklino, me doosh. to thiavatirio, sas?
You:	(offer your passport)
Receptionist:	Υπογράψτε εδώ, παρακαλώ
	ipograpste etho, parakalo
You:	(ask what time breakfast is served)

1.4 Practise saying these room numbers:

1.5 Order breakfast for the following people, using **θέλω**/the*lo* with the right form of the verb:

1 yourself (I) (tea with milk, eggs and bacon)
2 your son (he) (coffee, toast and jam)
3 all of you (we) (orange juice)
4 your daughter (she) (tea with lemon, toast, boiled egg)

2 DIRECTIONS

FINDING YOUR WAY AROUND

Museums There are many museums in Athens, and nearby famous archeological sites. The two not to miss in Athens are the National Archeological Museum, and the new Acropolis Museum on the site of the Parthenon.

It's a good idea to get a guide book and read up a little on ancient Greek history before you arrive.

Check regulations about photography – some museums allow you to take photographs as long as you don't use a flash. Others make a charge for flash photography.

2 DIRECTIONS

Που είναι η Ακρόπολη;
Where is the Acropolis?

Anne is checking her map of Athens. She asks the hotel receptionist for some help in getting to the Acropolis.

Anne: **Συγνώμη, που είναι η Ακρόπολη;** (showing her map)
signomi, poo ine i Acropoli?

Receptionist: **Είμαστε εδώ στο χάρτη στη γωνία. Η Ακρόπολη είναι**
imaste etho sto harti stin gonia. I Acropoli ine
εκεί. Στρίψτε δεξιά απο την πόρτα μας, και πάρτε το
eki. stripste theksia apo tin porta mas, ke parte to
δεύτερο δρόμο αριστερά.
theftero thromo aristera.

Anne: **Είναι μακριά με τα πόδια;**
ine makria me ta pothia?

Receptionist: Όχι, το πολύ δέκα λεπτά.
ohi, to poli theka lepta.

Anne: Ευχαριστώ. Η αρχαία Ελλάδα με περιμένει!
efharisto. i arhea elatha me perimeni!

2 DIRECTIONS

Words and phrases from the dialogue

Συγνώμη	*signomi*	Excuse me, sorry
Που είναι;	*poo ine*	Where is/are ...?
Εδώ	*etho*	here
Ο χάρτης	*o hartis*	map
Στο χάρτη	*sto harti*	on the map
Εκεί	*eki*	there
Στη γωνία	*stin gonia*	at the corner
Στρίψτε δεξιά	*stripste theksia*	turn right*
αριστερά	*aristera*	left
απο την πόρτα μας	*apo tin porta mas*	from our door/entrance
πάρτε το δεύτερο δρόμο	*parte to theftero thromo*	take the 2nd street ...
μακριά/κοντά	*makria/konda*	far/near
με τα πόδια	*me ta pothia*	on foot
το πολύ	*to poli*	at the most
δέκα λεπτά	*theka lepta*	ten minutes
Η Αρχαία Ελλάδα με περιμένει	*i arhea elatha me perimeni*	Ancient Greece awaits me!

*See page 38 for imperatives (giving orders).

Other useful words and phrases

η οδός	*i othos*	road/street (used in names/formal)
ο δρόμος	*o thromos*	road/street
το στενό	*to steno*	side street
η λεωφόρος	*i leoforos*	avenue
η πλατεία	*i platia*	square
το κέντρο	*to kendro*	centre
η στάση	*i stasi*	(bus) stop
απέναντι	*apenandi*	opposite
μετά ευθεία	*meta efthia*	afterwards straight on
Στην οδό ...	*stin otho ...*	into ... road/street

Που είναι το Τουριστικό Γραφείο;
poo ine to tooristiko grafio?
Where is the tourist office?

Έχετε χάρτη της πόλης;
ehete harti tis polis?
Do you have a map of the town?

Υπάρχει τράπεζα εδώ κοντά;
iparhi trapeza etho konda?
Is there a bank near here?

Πιο σιγά παρακαλώ, δεν καταλαβαίνω
pio siga parakalo, then katalaveno
Slower, please, I don't understand

Πέστε το ξανά, παρακαλώ
peste to ksana, parakalo
Say that again, please

ανοικτό	*anikto*	open	κλειστό	*klisto*	closed

2 MEETING PEOPLE

TALKING ABOUT YOURSELF

Απο που είστε;/Where are you from?

Anne is walking to the Acropolis and sees a couple ahead of her. She wants to check she is on the right road.

Anne: **Συγνώμη, αυτός είναι ο δρόμος για την Ακρόπολη;**
signomi – aftos ine o thromos ya tin akropoli?

Man: Ναι, δεσποινίς. Ελάτε μαζί μας. Και εμείς πηγαίνουμε εκεί.
ne, thespinis. elate mazi mas – ke emis piyenoome eki.

Woman: Απο που είστε;
apo poo iste?

Anne: **Είμαι απο την Αγγλία.**
ime apo tin anglia.

Man: Πόσο καιρό είστε στην Αθήνα;
posso kero iste stin athina?

Anne: Μόνο μία μέρα, **είναι η πρώτη επίσκεψή μου στην Ελλάδα.**
Mono mia mera, ine i proti episkepsi moo stin elatha.

As they walk up the steps to the Acropolis, Yiannis Vazakas introduces himself.

Yiannis: **Με λένε** Γιάννη Βαζάκα, (pointing to his wife)
me lene yanni vazaka.
Η γυναίκα μου, Ελένη.
i yineka moo, eleni.

Anne: **Χαίρω πολύ. Με** λένε Anne Johnson.
hero poli. me lene Anne Johnson.
Αγαπάω πολύ την ιστορία της Ελλάδας.
Agapao poli tin istoria tis Ellathas.

Yiannis: Αλήθεια; Εγώ είμαι αρχαιολόγος.
Alithea? Ego ime arheologos.

23

2 MEETING PEOPLE

Words and phrases from the dialogue

ο δρόμος για	o thromos ya	the road/street to ...
ελάτε μαζί μας	elate mazi mas	come with us
απο που είστε	apo poo iste	where are you from?
Είμαι απο την Αγγλία	ime apo tin anglia	I'm from England
η Αγγλία	i anglia	England
η Ελλάδα	i elatha	Greece
Πόσο καιρό είστε στην Ελλάδα;	posso kero iste stin elatha?	How long have you been in Greece?
μια μέρα	mia mera	one day
Η πρώτη επίσκεψή μου στην Ελλάδα	i proti episkepsi moo stin elatha	my first visit in/to Greece
Με λένε	me lene	my name is/I'm called
Η γυναίκα μου	i yineka moo	my wife
Χαίρω πολύ	hero poli?	how do you do?
Είμαι αρχαιολόγος	ime arheologos	I'm an archeologist

Making conversation

Τι δουλειά κάνετε;	ti thoolia kanete	What's your job? (= what work do you do?) see p. 94
Είμαι/Είμαστε εδώ για διακοπές	ime/imaste etho ya thiokopes	I'm/we're here on holiday
Είμαι εδώ για δουλειά	ime etho ya thoolia	I'm here on business
Είστε μόνος/μόνη σας	iste monos/moni sas	are you on your own?
Είμαι με τη γυναίκα μου	ime me ti yineka moo	I'm with my wife
τον άντρα μου	ton andra moo	husband
την οικογένειά μου	tin ikoyenia moo	family
μερικούς φίλους	merikoos filoos	some friends
Είμαι φοιτητής/φοιτήτρια	ime fititis/fititria	I'm a student (m/f)
Τι σπουδάζετε;	ti spoothazete?	What do you study?
Σπουδάζω ιατρική	spoothazo iatriki	I'm studying medicine
Είμαι Άγγλος	ime Anglos	I'm English (masc.)
Είμαι Αγγλίδα	ime Anglitha	I'm English (fem.)

2 MEETING PEOPLE

the way it works

Accusative case

As you saw in the Introduction, the word that is the object of a sentence is put into the accusative case in Greek. The ending of the word can change, depending on the gender, as well as the article that precedes it.

Singular

ο άνθρωπος	o anthropos	becomes **τον άνθρωπο**/ton anthropo
η μητέρα	i mitera	becomes **την μητέρα**/tin mitera
το παιδί	to pethi	remains the same in the accusative

Plural

οι άνθρωποι	i anthropi	becomes **τους ανθρώπους**/toos anthropoos
οι μητέρες	i miteres	becomes **τις μητέρες**/tis miteres
τα παιδιά	ta pethia	remains the same in the acc.

Prepositions

After prepositions (e.g. in, at, on) we use the accusative case.

Common Greek prepositions are

σε	se	in/at/to
απο	apo	from/out of
για	ya	for
με	me	with
μαζί με	mazi me	together with
μέχρι	mehri	until
χωρίς	horis	without
πριν	prin	before
μετά	meta	after

Σε/se combines with the definite article in the accusative case to produce **στη(ν)**/stin (fem.), **στο(ν)** (masc.), **στο** (neut.), e.g.:

στη γωνία	sti gonia	at the corner
στον πρώτο όροφο	ston proto orofo	on the first floor
στο πάρκο	sto parko	in the park

Agreement of adjectives

Adjectives always agree with the noun they qualify in terms of gender, number and case. In the dialogue Anne says **Η αρχαία Ελλάδα με περιμένει**/ i arhea elatha me perimeni. As **Ελλάδα**/elatha (Greece) is feminine, the adjective **αρχαία**/arhea (ancient) is also feminine.

With a masculine noun the same adjective would have the masculine ending **-ος**/-os, e.g. **Ο αρχαίος ναός**/o arheos naos (the ancient temple).

With a neuter noun the ending **-ο**/-o is used, e.g. **το αρχαίο κτίριο**/to arheo ktirio (the ancient building). **Το τουριστικό γραφείο**/To touristiko grafio (Travel Agency).

Note: the ending for the feminine adjective is either **-α**/-a, or **-η**/-i, e.g.:

| ωραία | orea | nice | μικρή | mikri | small |

2 MEETING PEOPLE

The genitive case

In the Introduction, the function of the genitive case was explained – to show ownership.

In Unit 1, Dialogue 4, you saw:

Ο αριθμός του δωματίου σας   the number of your room
o arithmos too thomatioo sas

Το δωμάτιο   *to thomatio* (nominative case) becomes
του δωματίου   *too thomatioo* (genitive case).

In this unit, Dialogue 3, you saw:

Αγαπάω πολύ την ιστορία της Ελλάδας   I love the history of Greece very much
agapao poli tin istoria tis elathas

Some more examples:

'John's key' in Greek would be   **Το κλειδί του Γιάννη**   *to klithi too Yanni*
'Mary's passport'   **Το διαβατήριο της Μαρίας**   *to thiavatirio tis Maria*
'The child's toy'   **Το παιχνίδι του παιδιού**   *to pehnithi too pethio*

things to do

2.1   Making conversation   You've met a very inquisitive Greek person, who wants to know all about you!

Greek: Απο που είστε;
You: (from England)
Greek: Τι δουλειά κάνετε;
You: (say what you do – see list page 94)
Greek: Είστε εδώ με την οικογένειά σας;
You: (yes, with your wife/husband/some friends)
Greek: Πόσο καιρό είστε στην Ελλάδα;
You: (three days)
Greek: Που μένετε;
You: (at the Hotel Acropolis)

2 PUBLIC TRANSPORT

TRAVELLING / MONEY AND TIME

Air   Athens Airport (near Glyfada, about 15 km outside the city) has two terminals: East (**Ανατολικό**/*anatoliko*) and West (**Δυτικό**/*thitiko*). East handles international airlines; West handles Olympic flights, both international and domestic, including the islands. You can transfer from one airport to the other by taxi. There is a bus service from the airports to Syntagma Square.

Bus   Greece has an excellent service of long distance buses that travel to all major cities and some islands like Zakynthos. In town buses are blue and white, and stop at blue bus stops. The standard fare of 75 drachmas is paid by buying a book of tickets from a kiosk, and inserting one ticket per journey in a stamping machine situated on the bus.

Trolleybus   Athens has a cheap and frequent trolleybus service – as with the buses, you must buy books of tickets from kiosks to use on board. Money does not change hands on trolleybuses. Trolley stops are yellow.

2 PUBLIC TRANSPORT

Electric train   The partially underground electric train service
(**ο ηλεκτρικός**/*elektrikos*) is a single line running north–south through
Athens from Kifisya to Pireus, via Omonia Square.

Taxis   No visit to Athens is complete without an exhilarating drive
in a Greek taxi! They are cheap, with a minimum charge of around a
pound. No need to tip, just round up to the nearest ten drachmas.
Look for the sign **ΕΛΕΥΘΕΡΟ**/*eleíthero* in the driver's window; if it is
raised, the taxi is free. At night, the taxi sign stays lit, even if the taxi is
occupied. Taxis will often take on several separate passengers en route if
they're going in the same direction. You often have to call out your
destination to the driver through the open right-hand window as he slows
down and passes you.

Athens also has a number of radio taxi companies – their telephone
numbers are always printed in *Athens News*.

In Athens during weekdays there can be traffic restrictions to reduce
exhaust pollution. Cars with even registration numbers can only circulate
in the inner ring (**δαχτύλιος**/*thaktilios*) on even number dates, and vice
versa. This used to apply to taxis, thus you'll sometimes see next to the
taxi sign on the roof of the car either the letter Z or M. These mean:

Ζυγός   *zigos*   even
Μονός   *monos*   odd

ΣΗΜΕΡΑ
ΚΥΚΛΟΦΟΡΟΥΝ
ΤΑ ΜΟΝΑ
ΑΥΡΙΟ
ΤΑ ΖΥΓΑ

2 PUBLIC TRANSPORT

Πηγαίνει αυτό το λεωφορείο στην πλάζ;
Does this bus go to the beach?

Peter decides to take the bus to go to the beach

Peter: **Συγνώμη, πηγαίνει αυτό το λεωφορείο στην πλάζ;**
        signomi – piyeni afto to leoforio stin plaj?

Driver: Ναι, φεύγει σε δέκα λεπτά.
        ne – fevyi se theka lepta.

Peter: **Πόσο κάνει το εισιτήριο;**
        posso kani to isitirio?

Driver: Ογδόντα δραχμές.
        ogthonda thrachmes.

Peter: **Σε ποιά στάση θα κατεβώ;**
        se pya stasi tha katevo?

Driver: **Στη Χρυσή Άμμο – θα σας πω.**
        sti hrisi amo – tha sas po.

2 PUBLIC TRANSPORT

Words and phrases from the dialogue

Πηγαίνει αυτό το λεωφορείο	piyeni afto to leoforio	Does this bus go ...?
στην πλάζ;	stin plaj	to the beach
φεύγει	fevyi	it leaves
σε πέντε λεπτά	se pende lepta	in five minutes
πόσο κάνει;	posso kani	How much is ...?*
το εισιτήριο;	to isitirio	the ticket
ογδόντα δραχμές	ogthonda thrachmes	80 drachmas (see p. 31)
σε ποιά στάση;	se pya stasi	(at) which stop ...?
Θα κατεβώ	tha katevo	I'll get off
Θα σας πω	tha sas po	I'll tell you
Στη Χρυσή Άμμο	sti hrisi amo	at 'Golden Sand'

* To say 'How much are ...?', the phrase changes to:
πόσο κάνουν;/*posso kanoon?*

Travel and transport signs

ΑΦΙΞΕΙΣ	AFIKSIS	arrivals
ΑΝΑΧΩΡΗΣΕΙΣ	ANAHORISIS	departures
ΠΛΗΡΟΦΟΡΙΕΣ	PLIROFORIES	information
ΤΕΛΩΝΕΙΟ	TELONIO	customs
ΕΛΕΓΧΟΣ	ELENHOS	passport
ΔΙΑΒΑΤΗΡΙΩΝ	THIAVATIRION	control
ΕΙΣΟΔΟΣ	ISOTHOS	entrance
ΕΞΟΔΟΣ	EXSOTHOS	exit

Other useful words and phrases

Τι ώρα έχει λεωφορείο/τρένο/πούλμαν/αεροπλάνο/πλοίο για ...
ti ora ehi leoforio/treno/pulman/aeroplano/plio ya ...
What time is there a bus, train, coach, plane, boat to ...?

Τι ώρα/πότε είναι το επόμενο/τελευταίο λεωφορείο για ...
ti ora/pote ine to epomeno/telefteo leoforio ya ...
What time is the next/last bus to ...?

Που μπορώ να πάρω ένα λεωφορείο για ...
poo boro na paro ena leoforio ya ...
Where can I get a bus to ...?

Το λεωφορείο είναι γεμάτο
to leoforio ine yemato
The bus is full

Πόση ώρα κάνει το λεωφορείο για ...
posi ora kani to leoforio ya ...
How long does the bus take to ...?

Είναι ελεύθερη (αυτή η θέση)
ine eleftheri (afti i thesi)
Is this seat free?

Πρέπει να αλλάξω (λεωφορείο);
prepi na alakso (leoforio)?
Do I have to change (buses)

Είναι το τρένο στην ώρα του;
ine to treno stin ora too?
Is the train on time?

Το αεροπλάνο έχει καθυστέρηση
to aeroplano ehi kathisterisi
The plane is delayed

2 PUBLIC TRANSPORT

GREEK MONEY

The drachma **δραχμή**/*thrahmi* is the name of the currency.
COINS: 1, 2, 5, 10, 20, 50, 100 drachmas **δραχμές**
NOTES: 50 (being phased out), 100, 500, 1000, 5000 drachmas

Numbers and money

30	τριάντα	*trianda*	100	εκατό	*ekato (n)*	(drachmas)
40	σαράντα	*saranda*	200	διακόσια	*thiakosia*	-es
50	πενήντα	*peninda*	300	τριακόσια	*triakosia*	-es
60	εξήντα	*eksinda*	400	τετρακόσια	*tetrakosia*	-es
70	εβδομήντα	*evthominda*	500	πεντακόσια	*pendakosia*	-es
80	ογδόντα	*ogthonda*	600	εξακόσια	*eksakosia*	-es
90	ενενήντα	*eneninda*	700	εφτακόσια	*eftakosia*	-es
			800	οκτακόσια	*oktakosia*	-es
			900	εννιακόσια	*enyakosia*	-es

1000	χίλια	hilia
	χίλιες	hilies (fem. for drachmas)
2000	δύο χιλιάδες	*thio hiliathes*
3000	τρεις χιλιάδες	*tris hiliathes*
4000	τέσσερις χιλιάδες	*tesseris hiliathes*

105	εκατόν πέντε	*ekaton pende*
124	εκατόν είκοσι τέσσερα	*ekaton ikosi tessera*

1675   χίλια εξακόσια εβδομήντα πέντε
        hilia eksakosia evthominda pende
        χίλιες εξακόσιες εβδομήντα πέντε δραχμές
        hilies eksakosies evthominda pende thrahmes

2 PUBLIC TRANSPORT

the way it works

Telling the time

Some basic words and phrases (see pages 15 and 31 for numbers):

η ώρα	*i ora*	hour
το λεπτό	*to lepto*	minute (plural **τα λεπτά**/*ta lepta*)
τι ώρα είναι;	*ti ora ine*	What time is it?
και τέταρτο	*ke tetarto*	quarter past
παρά τέταρτο	*para tetarto*	quarter to
και μισή	*ke misi*	half past
σε πέντε λεπτά	*se pende lepta*	in 5 minutes

Η ώρα είναι μία/δύο/τρείς/τέσσερις It's 1/2/3/4 o'clock
i ora ine mia/thio/tris/tesseris
στη μια/στις δύο/στις τρείς/στις τέσσερις at 1/2/3/4 o'clock
sti mia/stis thio/stis tris/stis tesseris
Είναι πέντε και τέταρτο/μισή It's quarter/half past five
ine pende ke tetarto/misi
Στις πέντε παρά τέταρτο At quarter to five
stis pende para tetarto

You may hear alternatives for half past the hour:

μιάμιση	*miamisi*	1.30
δυόμιση	*thiomisi*	2.30
τρεισήμιση	*trisimisi*	3.30
τεσσερεισήμιση	*teserisimi*	4.30
πεντέμιση	*pendemisi*	5.30

Note that the hour always comes first, and the minutes follow.

τρεις παρά είκοσι πέντε *tris para ikosi pende*
          or   2.35/twenty-five to three
δύο και τριάντα πέντε *thio ke trianda pende*

π.μ. (προ μεσημβρίας)	*pro mesimvrias*	a.m.
μ.μ. (μετά μεσημβρία)	*meta mesimvria*	p.m.

This and that

The words for this and that in Greek are **αυτός**/*aftos* this and **εκείνος**/*ekinos* that. These are adjectives and have to agree in number, case and gender with the noun to which they refer, e.g.:

αυτός ο δρόμος	*aftos o thromos*	this road
εκείνη η εκκλησία	*ekini i eklisia*	that church

Notice that you must use the definite article as well; literally you say 'this the road'.

2 PUBLIC TRANSPORT

Which? and Who?

The word for which/who? in Greek is

Ποιός	pyos	(masc.)
Ποιά	pya	(fem.)
Ποιό	pyo	(neut.)

Like **αυτός/εκείνος**/aftos/ekinos, these are also adjectives and have to agree with the noun to which they refer, e.g.:

Ποιό λεωφορείο πάει στην Ακρόπολη;   Which bus goes to the Acropolis?
pyo leoforio pai stin akropoli?

Ποιός είναι ο κύριος Σπύρου;   Who is Mr Spirou?
pyos ine o kirios Spiroo?

Masculine and feminine noun endings

On Monday you met some neuter nouns and their typical endings.

Feminine nouns have the following endings: **-η**/-i, **-α**/-a, e.g.:

η αδελφή   i athelfi   the sister
η θάλασσα   i thalassa   the sea

Masculine nouns have three typical endings: **-ος**/-os, **-ας**/-as, **-ης**/-is. e.g.:

ο δρόμος   o thromos   the road
ο άντρας   o andras   the man/husband
ο χάρτης   o hartis   the map

Table of noun endings

Here is a table of the endings you have met so far:

		nominative	accusative	genitive
Masculine	sing.	**-ος/-ας/-ης** -os/-as/-is	**-ο/-α/-η** -o/-a/-i	**-ου/-α/-η** -oo/-a/-i
	pl.	**-οι/-ες/-ες** -i/-es/-es	**-ους/-ες/-ες** -oos/-es/-es	**-ων/-ών/-ών** -on/-on/-on
Feminine	sing.	**-α/-η** -a/-i	**-α/-η** -a/-i	**-ας/-ης** -as/-is
	pl.	**-ες/-ες** -es/-es	**-ες/-ες** -es/-es	**-ων/-ών** -on/-on
Neuter	sing.	**-ο/-ι/-μα** -o/-i/-ma	**-ο/-ι/-μα** -o/-i/-ma	**-ου/-ου/-ματος** -oo/-oo/-matos
	pl.	**-α/-α/-ματα** -a/-a/-mata	**-α/-α/-ματα** -a/-a/-mata	**-ων/-ων/-ματων** -on/-on/-maton

2 PUBLIC TRANSPORT

things to do

2.2 Complete the sentences in Greek, and answer the questions, using the timetable opposite:

1 (What time/arrives) το πρώτο λεωφορείο;

2 Τι ώρα (leaves) το δεύτερο λεωφορείο;

3 (How long/takes) το λεωφορείο;

4 (How many buses go) στη Ραφήνα;

δρομολόγιο timetable το λεωφορείο για τη Ραφήνα bus to Rafina	
ΑΝΑΧΩΡΗΣΕΙΣ departure	**ΑΦΙΞΕΙΣ** arrival
9.15	10.30
10.45	12.15
12.15	13.45
14.30	16.00
16.15	17.45

2.3 Tell the times on the clocks shown, and the time of day – choose from the list given:

a.m.

1   03.00

2   08.30

3   11.55

p.m.

4   12.00

5   14.30

6   18.30

το πρωί   *to proi*
το απόγευμα   *to apoyevma*

το μεσημέρι   *to mesimeri*
το βράδυ   *to vrathi*

3 FOOD AND RESTAURANTS

EATING AND DRINKING

Going out for a drink   Greek cafes are open all day and evening, serving coffee, soft drinks, alcoholic drinks, sweets and ice-creams.

Greek coffee   As you'll see in the first dialogue, Greek coffee ελληνικός καφές/*elinikos kafes* comes in three types:

σκέτος	*sketos*	no sugar
μέτριος	*metrios*	medium sweet
γλυκός	*glikos*	sweet

Note in the dialogue that when you order, the coffee is in the accusative case, so the final -*s* is left off. For more than one coffee the plural ending becomes **-ους**/-*oos*, e.g. **δύο μέτριους**/*thio metrioos*.

The coffee grounds remain in the bottom half of the cup, so be careful not to swallow them! Coffee usually is accompanied by a welcoming glass of cold water – it's safe to drink. Bottled water is available everywhere.

You can also have instant coffee – called **νες**/*nes* (short for **νεσκαφέ**/*Nescafe*), either hot or cold. The latter is called **φραπέ**/*frappé*, and is served with ice and a straw.

Amstel is the local brand of beer, in half-litre bottles – foreign beers are increasingly available. Don't forget that **μπύρα**/*bira* is feminine, so you say **μια μπύρα**/*mia bira*. Plural **μπύρες**/*bires*.

Greek wines   Try **ρετσίνα**/*retsina*, the distinctive resinated wine of Greece (usually white) – it may taste strange at first, but it goes with everything! Available in bottles, or copper quarter, half and litre flasks. Try it with soda to make a longer drink.

Most people know **Δεμέστιχα**/*themestica* – red and white and rosé – always a good refreshing taste.

3 FOOD AND RESTAURANTS

Cheers!   To say 'cheers', simply raise your glass, clink it with everyone else's round the table and say **Στην υγειά μας**/*stin iyia mas* or **γειά μας**/*ya mas*. This literally means 'to our health'.

Στην υγειά σου/*stin iyia soo* or **γειά σου**/*ya soo*, means 'to your health'.

Asking for the bill   When you've finished your drink or meal, attract the waiter's attention by calling **κύριε**/*kirie*, or saying **παρακαλώ**/*parakalo*.

To ask for the bill, say **Το λογαριασμό, παρακαλώ**/*to logariasmo, parakalo*.

If you are a bit hesitant to speak, or the waiter is some distance away, do what most people do and, when you've caught his eye, make as if you are writing in the air. You'll soon be doing this like a native!

Tipping   Service is always included in the bill, so there is no need to add 10% automatically. Just round up what you give to the nearest 100 or 200 drachmas. If you have some coins·in change, leave them for the boy who clears away the table.

Φέρτε μας μια μπύρα/Bring us a beer

Peter got up late and is now settling down to one of life's great pleasures in Greece – sitting at a café and watching the world go by. It's hot but Peter wants to have a Greek coffee.

Waiter:	**Καλημέρα κύριε. Τι θα πάρετε;** *kalimera kirie. ti tha parete?*
Peter:	**Ένα καφέ, παρακαλώ.** *ena kafe parakalo.*
Waiter:	**Τι καφέ θέλετε, ελληνικό η νες;** *ti kafe thelete eliniko i nes?*
Peter:	**Δώστε μου ένα ελληνικό.** *thoste moo ena eliniko.*

3 FOOD AND RESTAURANTS

Waiter:	Σκέτο, μέτριο ή γλυκό;
	sketo, metrio i gliko?
Peter:	Μέτριο παρακαλώ.
	metrio parakalo.
Waiter:	Αμέσως.
	amesos.

At the next table ...

Kostas:	Κάνει πολύ ζέστη σήμερα. Διψάω πολύ.
	kani poli zesti simera. thipsao poli.
Maria:	Κύριε, φέρτε μας μία παγωμένη
	kirie, ferte mas mia pagomeni
	μπύρα και μια πορτοκαλάδα.
	bira ke mia portokalatha.
Waiter:	Μάλιστα.
	malista.
Peter:	Συγνώμη, έχετε φωτιά ..;
	signomi, ehete fotya ..?

Words and phrases from the dialogue

Τι θα πάρετε;	*ti tha parete*	What will you have (take)?
Δώστε μου	*thoste moo*	give me
Φέρτε μου	*ferte moo*	bring me
αμέσως	*amesos*	at once/straight away
Κάνει πολύ ζέστη	*kani poli zesti*	it's very hot (weather)
σήμερα	*simera*	today
Διψάω	*thipsao*	I'm thirsty
μια μπύρα	*mia bira*	a beer (lager type)
παγωμένος -η -ο	*pagomenos -i -o*	cold/chilled
μια πορτοκαλάδα	*mia portokalatha*	an orangeade (fizzy)
μάλιστα	*malista*	of course
Έχετε φωτιά;	*ehete fotya*	do you have a light ...?

Drinks and Snacks

ο καπουτσίνο	*o kapootsino*	capuccino
ο εσπρέσσο	*o espreso*	espresso
η λεμονάδα	*i lemonatha*	lemonade
η κόκα-κόλα	*i koka-kola*	coca-cola
η σόδα	*i sotha*	soda
το ούζο	*to oozo*	ouzo
το κονιάκ	*to koniak*	brandy
το κρασί	*to krasi*	wine
κόκκινο	*kokino*	red
άσπρο	*aspro*	white
ροζέ	*roze*	rosé
το παγωτό	*to pagoto*	ice-cream
η πάστα	*i pasta*	cake
ο μπακλαβάς	*o baklavas*	baclava
το σάντουϊτς	*to sandooits*	sandwich

Που είναι οι τουαλέττες; *poo ine i tooaletes* where are the toilets?

3 FOOD AND RESTAURANTS

Talking about the weather

τι καιρό κάνει;	ti kero kani	what's the weather like?
Ο καιρός είναι καλός	o keros ine kalos	the weather is good
άσκημος	askimos	bad
κάνει κρύο/ζέστη	kani krio/zesti	it's cold/hot
έχει ήλιο	ehi ilio	it's sunny
έχει συννεφιά	ehi sinefia	it's cloudy
βρέχει	vrehi	it's raining
φυσάει	fisai	it's windy
ο καύσωνας	o kafsonas	heatwave
το δελτίο καιρού	to theltio keroo	weather forecast
Η θάλασσα είναι ήσυχη	i thalasa ine isihi	the sea is calm
ταραγμένη	taragmeni	rough
Έχει δροσιά	ehi throsia	it's cool

the way it works

Orders and instructions

In the first dialogue Peter tells the waiter to give him a Greek coffee (by the way, in Greece you can be quite direct with orders, and don't need the 'politeness' of, e.g. the English 'could I please have . . .'). The grammatical term for an order is the imperative.

This is how some common Greek verbs form their imperative:

First person present		Polite/Plural imperative		
φέρνω	ferno	φέρτε	ferte	bring
πηγαίνω	piyeno	πηγαίνετε	piyenete	go
δίνω	thino	δώστε	thoste	give
έρχομαι	erhome	ελάτε	elate	come
κάθομαι	kathome	καθίστε	kathiste	sit
παίρνω	perno	πάρτε	parte	take
περιμένω	perimeno	περιμένετε	perimenete	wait
αφήνω	afino	αφήστε	afiste	leave
λέω	leo	πέστε	peste	say
στρίβω	strivo	στρίψτε	stripste	turn
περνάω	pernao	περάστε	peraste	pass
δοκιμάζω	thokimazo	δοκιμάστε	thokimaste	try

Verbs ending in -άω/-ao

Unlike θέλω/thelo, κάνω/kano, ξέρω/ksero, καταλαβαίνω/katalaveno, there is a group of verbs which end in -αω/-ao in the first person singular present tense. In this unit you've met διψάω/thipsao – I'm thirsty – and will meet πεινάω/pinao – I'm hungry – later.

Another useful verb is μιλάω/milao, I speak.

3 FOOD AND RESTAURANTS

Here are the present tense endings:

-άω	-ao	**μιλάω**	*milao*	I speak
-άς	-as	**μιλάς**	*milas*	you speak
-άει	-ai	**μιλάει**	*milai*	he/she speaks
-άμε	-ame	**μιλάμε**	*milame*	we speak
-άτε	-ate	**μιλάτε**	*milate*	you speak
-άν(ε)	-ane	**μιλάν(ε)**	*milane*	they speak

Μιλάτε Ελληνικά; Ναι, μιλάω λίγο
milate elinika? ne, milao ligo
Διψάς Μαρία; Ναι, θέλω ένα ποτήρι νερό, παρακαλώ
thipsas Maria? ne, thelo ena potiri nero parakalo

Do you speak Greek?
Yes, I speak a little
Are you thirsty, Maria?
Yes, I want a glass of
water, please

Eating out

Greece is full of every variety of eating place, from the street seller
of grilled ears of corn, or bread sticks (*koulouria*), to the smartest
hotel restaurant. Although fast food places are springing up
everywhere, the traditional eating place is the taverna – usually a
simple, no-fuss family restaurant with a limited menu of dishes.

The normal thing to do when you go to a taverna is to go into the
kitchen and select what you want to eat – if you're having fish, you
can have it weighed and a price quoted.

Incidentally the best fast food in Greece is the *souvlaki* (**σουβλάκι**), a
few skewers of pork pieces in pitta bread with salad, bought from a
small snack bar on the street. They are delicious and filling.

Most Greeks have a late lunch around 1.30/2.00 pm, a siesta for a few
hours, then back to work, before a late-night supper around 9 pm or
10 pm.

On the road, you'll see grill houses called **Ψησταριά**/*psistaria*, where
a limited range of grilled meat dishes is available.

Larger restaurants are called **Εστιατόριο**/*estiatorio*, where a wider
range of dishes is available.

3 FOOD AND RESTAURANTS

Πάμε μαζί/Let's go together

Peter wants to find somewhere to eat, and asks his new friends for a recommendation.

Peter: **Κώστα, υπάρχει μία καλή ταβέρνα εδώ κοντά;**
Kosta, iparhi mia kali taverna etho konda

Costas: **Ναι, βέβαια. Υπάρχει μια πολύ καλή. Την λένε τα "Τρία αδέλφια"**
ne vevea. iparhi mia poli kali. tin lene ta tria athelfia
Τρώμε εκεί σχεδόν κάθε βράδυ
trome eki skethon kathe vrathi

Maria: **Πάμε μαζί απόψε;**
pame mazi apopse?

Costas: **Μαρία, δεν ξέρω ...**
Maria, then ksero ...

Peter: **Θαυμάσια ιδέα. Τι ώρα λοιπόν;**
thavmasia ithea. ti ora lipon?

Words and phrases from the dialogue

Υπάρχει ...;	*iparhi*	is there ...?
Υπάρχουν ...;	*iparhoon*	are there ...?
Εδώ κοντά	*etho konda*	near here
Βέβαια	*vevea*	absolutely
Τα Τρία Αδέλφια	*Ta tria Adelfia*	''The Three Brothers''
τρώμε εκεί	*trome eki*	we eat there
σχεδόν	*skethon*	nearly
κάθε βράδυ	*kathe vrathi*	every evening
πάμε μαζί	*pame mazi*	let's go together
απόψε	*apopse*	tonight
δεν ξέρω	*then ksero*	I don't know
θαυμάσια ιδέα	*thavmasia ithea*	great idea
τι ώρα	*ti ora*	what time?
λοιπόν	*lipon*	well/anyway/now then

Ένα τραπέζι για τρεις;/A table for three?

Peter, Maria and Costas meet at the Three Brothers taverna.

Waiter: **Καλησπέρα σας. Ένα τραπέζι για τρεις;**
kalispera sas. ena trapezi ya tris?

Maria: **Ναι, ένα καλό τραπέζι για τον Άγγλο μας.**
ne ena kalo trapezi ya ton anglo mas.

Kostas: **Μας δίνετε τον κατάλογο, παρακαλώ.**
mas thinete ton katalogo, parakalo.

Maria: **Φέρτε μας μερικούς μεζέδες πρώτα. Ένα τζατζίκι, μιά**
ferte mas merikous mezethes prota. ena tzaziki, mia
ταραμοσαλάτα και μια χωριάτικη.
taramosalata ke mia horiatiki.

3 FOOD AND RESTAURANTS

Costas: **Τι ψάρια έχετε;**
ti psaria ehete?

Waiter: Έχουμε ξιφία, μπαρμπούνια και καλαμαράκια.
ehoome ksifia, barboonya ke kalamarakya.

Maria: Peter, προτιμάς ψάρι ή κρέας;
Peter, protimas psari i kreas?

Peter: Κρέας νομίζω. Πεινάω σαν λύκος. Μ' αρέσει πολύ το σουβλάκι.
kreas nomizo. pinao san likos. m' aresi poli to soovlaki.

Waiter: Είστε έτοιμοι;
iste etimi?

Maria: Ναι. Λοιπόν, **θα πάρουμε ένα σουβλάκι, μια καλαμαράκια,**
ne. lipon tha paroome ena soovlaki, mia kalamarakya,
ένα ξιφία και δύο πατάτες τηγανητές.
ena ksifia ke thio patates tiganites.

Waiter: Τι θα πιείτε;
ti tha pyite?

Costas: **Φέρτε μας ένα μπουκάλι ρετσίνα.** Ελληνικό φαγητό χωρίς κρασί!;
ferte mas ena bookali retsina (turning to the others) *eliniko fagito horis krasi!?*

Cheval!

ΑΧΑΡΝΩΝ 282
ΠΙΤΣΑΡΙΑ-ΕΣΤΙΑΤΟΡΙΟ
ΤΗΛ. 864 2258

ΤΟ CHEVAL ΚΑΘΕ ΜΕΡΑ, ΜΕΣΗΜΕΡΙ ΚΑΙ ΒΡΑΔΥ
ΣΑΣ ΠΡΟΣΦΕΡΕΙ ΜΙΑ ΜΕΓΑΛΗ ΠΟΙΚΙΛΙΑ ΦΑΓΗΤΩΝ,
ΣΕ ΦΘΗΝΕΣ ΤΙΜΕΣ ΚΑΙ ΓΡΗΓΟΡΗ ΕΞΥΠΗΡΕΤΗΣΗ.

ΤΙΜΟΚΑΤΑΛΟΓΟΣ ΓΙΑ ΤΟ ΣΠΙΤΙ

ΠΙΤΣΕΣ

ΤΥΡΙ, σάλτσα	530
ΖΑΜΠΟΝ, τυρί, σάλτσα	550
(και όλες οι πίτσες μ' ένα είδος)	550
ΖΑΜΠΟΝ, μπέικον, τυρί, σάλτσα	580
(και όλες οι πίτσες μ' ένα είδος)	580
ΤΟΝΟΣ, κλπ.	600
SPECIAL (απ' όλα)	600
SUPER SPECIAL	620

ΖΥΜΑΡΙΚΑ

ΝΑΠΟΛΙ σάλτσα, τυρί, σπαγγέτι, λαζάνια	210
ΜΠΟΛΩΝΕΖ σάλτσα, τυρί, σπαγγέτι, λαζάνια	300
SPECIAL μακαρόνια, ζαμπόν, μπέικον, μανιτάρια	320
RIGATONI 4 τυριά	370
ΚΑΝΕΛΛΟΝΙΑ	400
ΒΟΥΤΥΡΟΥ σπαγγέτι, λαζάνια	180

ΣΑΛΑΤΕΣ

ΡΑΨΩΔΙΑ μικρή	320
ΡΑΨΩΔΙΑ μεγάλη	400
ΧΩΡΙΑΤΙΚΗ	220
ΛΑΧΑΝΟΚΗΠΟΣ	220
ΡΟΖ ΣΑΛΑΤΑ	260
ΠΡΑΣΙΝΗ ΣΑΛΑΤΑ	140
ΚΟΚΚΙΝΗ, άσπρη, εποχής	240
ΡΩΣΣΙΚΗ	150
ΠΑΤΑΤΟΣΑΛΑΤΑ	150
ΜΕΛΙΤΖΑΝΟΣΑΛΑΤΑ	150
ΤΖΑΤΖΙΚΙ	150

ΔΙΑΦΟΡΑ

ΜΑΝΙΤΑΡΙΑ τηγανητά	300
ΠΑΤΑΤΕΣ	90
ΤΥΡΙ φέτα	130
ΡΟΚΦΟΡ	170
ΚΕΦΑΛΟΓΡΑΒΙΕΡΑ	160

ΤΗΣ ΩΡΑΣ

ΜΠΙΦΤΕΚΙ σχάρας	360
ΜΠΙΦΤΕΚΙ chef, Cheval	440
ΜΠΙΦΤΕΚΙ με αυγά	460
ΣΥΚΩΤΙ σχάρας	450
ΦΙΛΕΤΟ σχάρας	640
ΧΟΙΡΙΝΗ - ΜΟΣΧΑΡΙΣΙΑ σχάρας	460
ΣΟΥΒΛΑΚΙ	520
ΣΑΓΑΝΑΚΙ	320
ΟΜΕΛΕΤΕΣ διάφορες	280
ΟΜΕΛΕΤΕΣ complé	320
ΣΑΝΤΟΥΙΤΣ	160
ΠΑΣΤΕΣ	125

Restaurant menu items

τζατζίκι	*tzatziki*	yoghurt, cucumber, garlic dip
χωριάτικη	*horiatiki*	country salad, with feta cheese
καλαμαράκια	*kalamarakia*	little squids, fried whole
ξιφίας	*ksifias*	swordfish
μπαρμπούνια	*barboonya*	red mullet – usually priced by the kilo, which is enough for 3/4 people

3 FOOD AND RESTAURANTS

Words and phrases from the dialogue

ένα τραπέζι για τρεις	ena trapezi ya tris	a table for three
για τον Άγγλο μας	ya ton anglo mas	for our Englishman
μας δίνετε	mas thinete	give us
ο κατάλογος	o katalogos	the menu
μερικοί -ές -ά	meriki/es/a	some
μεζέδες	mezethes	starters
πρώτα	prota	first
τι ψάρια έχετε ;	ti psaria ehete	what fish do you have?
προτιμάς ... ή ...	protimas ... i ...	do you prefer ... or ... ?
κρέας	kreas	meat
νομίζω	nomizo	I think
πεινάω (σαν λύκος)	pinao (san likos)	I'm hungry (as a wolf)
μ΄ αρέσει	m΄ aresi	I like (sing.)
μ΄ αρέσουν	m΄ aresoon	I like (plural)
το σουβλάκι	to soovlaki	kebab
είστε έτοιμοι;	iste etimi	are you ready?
θα πάρουμε	tha paroome	we'll take/have ...
πατάτες τηγανητές	patates tiganites	chips (fried potatoes)
Τι θα πιείτε;	ti tha pyite?	what will you drink?
ένα μπουκάλι ρετσίνα	ena bookali retsina	a bottle of retsina
το ελληνικό φαγητό	to eliniko fagito	Greek food
χωρίς	horis	without
το κρασί	to krasi	wine

Other useful phrases

μπορώ να κλείσω ένα τραπέζι;	boro na kliso ena trapezi?	Can I book a table?
μπορώ να δω τι έχετε;	boro na tho ti ehete?	Can I see what you have?
Ελάτε στην κουζίνα	elate stin koozina	Come into the kitchen
πιάτο της ημέρας	piato tis imeras	dish of the day
κουβέρ	koover	cover charge
μπορώ να παραγγείλω;	boro na parangilo?	Can I order?
Λίγο νερό, παρακαλώ	ligo nero parakalo	Some water, please
ορεκτικά	orektika	starters
κύριο πιάτο	kirio piato	main course
επιδόρπιο	epithorpio	dessert
Το λογαριασμό, παρακαλώ	to logariasmo, parakalo	The bill, please
Μου εξηγείτε το λογαριασμό;	moo eksiyite to logariasmo?	Can you explain the bill?
Μήπως κάνατε λάθος	mipos kanate lathos	Maybe you've made a mistake

See topic vocabulary, pages 98–100, for names of food, drink, vegetables, etc.

the way it works

Personal pronouns

On Monday you saw the nominative (subject form of the noun) forms of the personal pronouns, e.g.: **Εγώ**/*ego*, **εσύ**/*esi*. In the first dialogue, **μου**/*moo* and **μας**/*mas* (me and us) in **δώστε μου**/*thoste moo* and **φέρτε μας**/*ferte mas*, are in the genitive case. This case is used after verbs like give, bring, tell, etc. (where we often use 'to' in English) as well as signifying possession (see the Introduction and Tuesday, page 26).

Here is a complete table of all the personal pronouns in the three cases:

nominative		accusative		(longer form)	genitive	
εγώ	ego	με/(ε)μένα	me	(e)mena	μου	moo
εσύ	esi	σε/(ε)σένα	se	(e)sena	σου	soo
αυτός	aftos	τον/αυτόν	ton	afton	του	too
αυτή	afti	την/αυτήν	tin	aftin	της	tis
αυτό	afto	το/αυτο	to	afto	του	too
εμείς	emis	μας/(ε)μάς	mas	(e)mas	μας	mas
εσείς	esis	σας/(ε)σάς	sas	(e)sas	σας	sas
αυτοί	afti	τους/αυτούς	toos	aftoos	τους	toos
αυτές	aftes	τις/αυτές	tis	aftes	τους	toos
αυτά	afta	τα/αυτά	ta	afta	τους	toos

Examples:

Την περιμένω στη στάση κάθε πρωί   I wait for her at the bus stop
tin perimeno sti stasi kathe proi   every morning
Τους βλέπω κάθε μέρα   I see them every day
toos vlepo kathe mera

Note the position of the personal pronoun before the verb.

After a preposition like **για**/*ya* (for), the longer form of the accusative personal pronoun is used.

Η μπύρα είναι για μένα, η πορτοκαλάδα είναι για αυτήν   The beer is for me, the
i bira ine ya mena, i portokalatha ine ya aftin   orangeade is for her
Δώστε του τον καφέ   Give him the coffee
thoste too ton kafe
Συγνώμη, φέρτε μου κι ένα παγωτό   Sorry, bring me an
Signomi, ferte moo ke ena pagoto   ice-cream as well

3 FOOD AND RESTAURANTS

things to do

3.1 Order the following coffees and cold drinks:

1   medium

2   plain   sweet

3   2 medium

4   a beer

5   2 beers

6   3 cokes

3.2 Try and complete this dialogue in a cafe

You: (The bill, please)
Waiter: **Μάλιστα, δύο μπύρες και δύο τόστ.**
     malista thio bires ke thio tost.
You: (say you're sorry, but the order is 2 beers, 1 toast)
Waiter: **Λυπάμαι, έχετε δίκιο.**
     lipame, ehete thikio.
You: (ask how much)
Waiter: **Τρείς χιλιάδες εξακόσιες δραχμές.**
     tris hiliathes eksakosies thrahmes.
You: (offer 4000 dr and say he can keep the change).

3.3 Try to complete this dialogue in a restaurant:

ΚΑΤΑΛΟΓΟΣ
MENU

ΟΡΕΚΤΙΚΑ

Καλαμαράκια	1200 δρχ
Χταπόδι	1250
Ταραμοσαλάτα	900
Τζατζίκι	900
Χωριάτικη	1200
Πατάτες τηγανητές	800

ΨΑΡΙΑ

Ξιφίας	1500
Μπαρμπούνια (το κιλό)	8000

ΚΡΑΣΙΑ

Δεμέστιχα	1500 δρχ
Ρετσίνα	1200
Μπύρα	600
Κόκα κόλα	400
Σόδα	300

Waiter: **Είστε έτοιμοι;**
     iste etimi?
You: (1 squid, 1 octopus, 1 tara)
Waiter: **Και μετά;**
     ke meta?
You: (half kilo of red mullet, and two portions of chips)
Waiter: **Εντάξει. Τι θα πιείτε;**
     endaksi, ti tha pyite?
You: (bottle of retsina and 1 soda)
Waiter: **Αμέσως.**
     amesos.
You: (and a Greek salad, please)
Waiter: **Εντάξει.**
     endaksi.

If your maths is good, add up your order and say how much your bill is in Greek money!

3 BANK AND POST OFFICE

CHANGING MONEY / BUYING STAMPS

Banks and exchanges Look for the word **ΤΡΑΠΕΖΑ**/*trapeza*, which means bank, and **ΣΥΝΑΛΛΑΓΜΑ**/*synalagma*, which means exchange.

Banking hours in the city are usually 8.00 am–2.00 pm Mondays to Thursdays; 8.00 am–1.30 pm Fridays.

For rapid 24-hour counter service in Athens, go to the National Bank of Greece (**ΕΘΝΙΚΗ ΤΡΑΠΕΖΑ ΤΗΣ ΕΛΛΑΔΟΣ/***ethniki trapeza tis elathos*) in Constitution (*Syntagma*) Square.

To change travellers cheques you'll need your passport. In most banks a clerk will carry out the transaction, then you go to a separate cash desk (**ΤΑΜΕΙΟ**/*tamio*) to get your money.

On the islands there are often many exchange offices available, as well as banks, that are open mornings and evenings.

3 BANK AND POST OFFICE

θέλω να χαλάσω εκατό λίρες
I want to change £100

Anne wants to change some travellers cheques and send postcards home. She first goes to the bank.

Clerk: Παρακαλώ.
parakalo.

Anne: **Θέλω να χαλάσω μερικά travellers cheques.**
thelo na halaso merika travellers cheques.

Clerk: Πόσα τσέκ έχετε;
Posa chek ehete?

Anne: **Δύο τσέκ εκατό λίρες το καθένα. Διακόσιες λίρες.**
thio chek ekato lires to kathena. thiakosies lires.

Clerk: **Το διαβατήριό σας παρακαλώ. Ποιά είναι η διεύθυνσή σας;**
to thiavatirio sas parakalo – pya ine i thiefthinsi sas?

Anne: Μένω στο ξενοδοχείο Ακρόπολη οδός Μητσαίων δέκα εφτά.
meno sto ksenothohio akropoli othos mitseon theka efta.

Clerk: Υπογράψτε εδώ, και μετά πηγαίνετε στο ταμείο απέναντι.
ipograpste etho, ke meta piyenete sto tamio apenandi.

Anne: Εντάξει ευχαριστώ. Συγνώμη, που είναι το ταχυδρομείο;
endaksi efharisto. signomi poo ine to tahithromio?

Words and phrases from the dialogue

Μερικά	*merika*	some
Θέλω να χαλάσω	*thelo na halaso*	I want to change
Πόσα τσέκ έχετε;	*posa chek ehete*	How many cheques have you got?
εκατό λίρες το καθένα	*ekato lires to kathena*	£100 each
το διαβατήριό σας	*to thiavatirio sas*	your passport
η διεύθυνσή σας	*i thiefthinsi sas*	your address
Υπογράψτε εδώ	*ipograpste etho*	sign here
πηγαίνετε	*piyenete*	go
το ταμείο	*to tamio*	cash desk
απέναντι	*apenandi*	opposite
Μένω ... οδός	*Meno ... othos*	I'm living/staying ...
Μητσαίων 17	*Mitseon 17*	17 Mitseon Street
το ταχυδρομείο	*to tahithromio*	post office

3 BANK AND POST OFFICE

πιστωτική κάρτα	*pistotiki karta*	credit card
το νόμισμα	*to nomisma*	coin
το χαρτονόμισμα	*to hartonomisma*	banknote
το τσέκ/η επιταγή	*to chek/i epitayi*	cheque
το βιβλίο επιταγών	*to vivlio epitagon*	chequebook
Πόσο έχει η λίρα σήμερα;	*poso ehi i lira simera*	what's the rate of the pound today?

Συμπληρώστε αυτό το έντυπο
simbliroste afto to endipo
Θέλω να πάρω μερικά λεφτά με Access
thelo na paro merika lefta me Access
Που να υπογράψω;
poo na ipograpso

fill out this form

I want to draw some money
   on Access
Where do I sign?

Μου δίνετε γραμματόσημα;
Give me some stamps

Anne goes to the post office.

Anne: Θέλω να στείλω έξη κάρτες στην Αγγλία. **Μου δίνετε**
   thelo na stilo eksi kartes stin anglia. moo thinete
   γραμματόσημα παρακαλώ;
   gramatosima parakalo?

Clerk: Μάλιστα. Έξι γραμματόσημα εξήντα δραχμές το ένα.
   malista. eksi gramatosima eksinda thrahmes to ena.
   Τριακόσιες εξήντα δραχμές όλα μαζί.
   triakosies eksinda thrahmes ola mazi.

Anne: Εντάξει. Ορίστε.
   endaksi. oriste.

Clerk: Ορίστε τα ρέστα σας.
   oriste ta resta sas.

Anne: **Συγνώμη, θέλω να τηλεφωνήσω στην Αγγλία.**
   Signomi, thelo na tilefoniso stin anglia.

ΤΑΧΥΔΡΟΜΙΚΟΝ
ΤΑΜΙΕΥΤΗΡΙΟΝ

3 BANK AND POST OFFICE

Words and phrases from the dialogue

θέλω να στείλω	th*elo na stilo*	I want to send
έξι κάρτες	*eksi kartes*	6 postcards
το γραμματόσημο -α	*to gramatosimo -a*	stamp -s
όλα μαζί	*ola mazi*	all together
τα ρέστα σας	*ta resta sas*	your change
θέλω να τηλεφωνήσω	th*elo na tilefoniso*	I want to telephone

Other useful phrases

το γράμμα/τα γράμματα	*to grama/ta gramata*	letter/s
ο φάκελλος	*o fakelos*	envelope
το δέμα/τα δέματα	*to thema/ta themata*	parcel/s
το στυλό	*to stilo*	ball point pen
το γραμματοκιβώτιο	*to gramatokivotio*	letterbox
αεροπορικώς	*aeroporikos*	by air mail
συστημένο	*sistimeno*	registered
τι ώρα ανοίγει;	*ti ora aniyi*	What time does it open?
κλείνει;	*klini*	close?
Για που είναι;	*ya poo ine*	Where is it/are they for?
Σε ποιό γκισέ;	*se pyo gise*	At which counter ...?

For notes on telephoning, see page 79.

the way it works

I want to ...

θέλω να ...   th*elo na* ...   I want to ...

After **θέλω να**/th*elo na* ..., you will find a different form of the verb used. Notice how in the dialogue Anne says **θέλω να χαλάσω**/th*elo na halaso* – for 'I want to change ...'. In the present tense form the verb would normally be **χαλάω**/*halao*.

See also page 66 for the future with **θα**/th*a* which uses the same form.

things to do

3.4   At the bank

Put the sentences of this dialogue in the right order:

a   Μάλιστα. Η λίρα έχει 390 δραχμές σήμερα.
b   Που είναι το συνάλλαγμα;
c   Ορίστε – μένω στο ξενοδοχείο "Όμηρος"
d   Το διαβατήριό σας και τη διεύθυνσή σας, παρακαλώ.
e   Απέναντι, κύριε, δεξιά.
f   Θέλω να χαλάσω εκατό λίρες.

4 SHOPPING

IN SHOPS AND MARKETS

Shop opening hours vary from day to day in the summer months (June to mid-September):

Monday	8.30 or 9.00 am – 2.30 or 3.00 pm	Thursday	8.30 or 9.00 am – 1.30 pm; 5.00 pm – 8.00 pm
Tuesday	8.30 or 9.00 am – 1.30 pm; 5.00 pm – 8.00 pm	Friday	8.30 or 9.00 am – 1.30 pm; 5.00 pm – 8.00 pm
Wednesday	8.30 or 9.00 am – 2.30 or 3.00 pm	Saturday	8.30 or 9.00 am – 2.30 or 3.00 pm

Supermarkets are open 8.30 am – 8.30 pm daily except Sunday.

In resort locations and the islands, shops will have more flexible hours, with souvenir shops, supermarkets, jewellers and chemists open until 10.00 pm or later.

In Greece cheques and chequebooks are a rarity. Most people use cash for transactions. Tourist shops and restaurants, however, increasingly take credit and charge cards like Access, Visa, American Express.

Plaka – 'flea market'   The most famous shopping area for souvenirs, leather, jewellery and reproductions of ancient art is the Plaka – at the foot of the Acropolis – easily reached from Syntagma Square. One area, next to the Monastiraki metro station, is called the Flea Market, where antique dealers and bargain-hunters abound.

The main shopping areas of Athens are in Ermou Street (off Syntagma Square), especially for leather, shoes, furs; Stadiou and Panepistimiou. For boutiques and high fashion, then Kolonaki Square is for you. It's also the place where the 'beautiful people' go to be seen!

4 SHOPPING

BUYING FOOD

Δώστε μου ένα κιλό/Give me a kilo

Anne is taking the bus to Sounio today and wants to buy food for a
picnic on the beach. Her first stop is the bakers (**ο φούρνος**/
o foornos).

Baker: Καλημέρα σας κυρία. Παρακαλώ;
kalimera sas kiria. parakalo?

Anne: **Μια φραντζόλα μαύρο ψωμί παρακαλώ.** Μήπως έχετε
τυρόπιττες;
mia franjola mavro psomi parakalo. mipos ehete tiropites?

Baker: Βεβαίως. Εδώ είναι κυρία. Είναι πολύ φρέσκιες.
veveos. etho ine kiria. ine poli freskies.

Anne: Δώστε μου δύο. **Πόσο κάνουν;**
thoste moo thio. posso kanoon?

Baker: Εκατόν σαράντα δραχμές.
ekatov saranta thrahmes.

Anne then goes to the greengrocers.

Assistant: Ορίστε. Τι φρούτα
oriste. ti froota
θέλετε;
thelete?

Anne: Μ' αρέσουν πολύ τα
m' aresoon poli ta
ροδάκινα. Δώστε μου
rothakina. thoste moo
ένα κιλό.
ena kilo.

Assistant: Θέλετε απο αυτά ή
thelete apo afta i
απο εκείνα;
apo ekina?

Anne: Προτιμώ τα μικρά. Θα
protimo ta mikra. tha
ήθελα και μισό κιλό
ithela ke miso kilo
σταφύλια.
stafilia.

Assistant: Τα μαύρα είναι πιο γλυκά. Δοκιμάστε τα.
ta mavra ine pyo glika. thokimaste ta.

Anne: Ναι, έχετε δίκιο. **Θα πάρω λοιπόν μισό κιλό μαύρα.**
ne ehete thikio. tha paro lipon miso kilo mavra.
Πόσο είναι;
poso ine?

4 SHOPPING

Assistant:	Πεντακόσιες σαράντα. Δεν έχετε ψιλά;
	pendakosies saranda. then ehete psila?
Anne:	Για να δω. Δυστυχώς δεν έχω.
	ya na tho. thistihos then eho.
Assistant:	Καλά. Δεν πειράζει. Ορίστε τα ρέστα σας.
	kala then birazi. oriste ta resta sas.

Words and phrases from the dialogue

ροδάκινα	*rothakina*	peaches
μια φραντζόλα	*mia franjola*	a loaf
μαύρο ψωμί	*mavro psomi*	brown bread
μήπως έχετε;	*mipos ehete*	do you have perhaps?
μια τυρόπιττα -ες	*mia tiropita -es*	cheese pie/ies
φρέσκιες	*freskies*	fresh (fem./plur.)
Δώστε μου	*thoste moo*	give me
απο αυτά ή απο εκείνα	*apo afta i apo ekina*	from these or those
Θα ήθελα	*tha ithela*	I'd like
μισό κιλό σταφύλια	*miso kilo stafilia*	half a kilo of grapes
πιο ... απο ...	*pyo ... apo ...*	more ... than ...
δοκιμάστε τα	*thokimaste ta*	try them
έχετε δίκιο	*ehete thikio*	you're right
δεν έχετε ψιλά;	*then ehete psila*	don't you have change?
Για να δω	*ya na tho*	I'll see
δυστυχώς	*thistihos*	unfortunately
δεν πειράζει	*then birazi*	it doesn't matter
Προτιμώ τα μικρά	*protimo ta mitra*	I prefer the small ones
τα μαύρα	*ta mavra*	the black ones (grapes)

Other useful words and phrases

Είναι φρέσκο -α;	*ine fresco -a*	is it fresh?
Τι είναι αυτό/αυτά;	*ti ine afto/afta*	what's this/these?
ένα τέταρτο	*ena tetarto*	quarter (kilo)
ένα λίτρο	*ena litro*	litre
ένα πακέτο	*ena paketo*	packet
μία κονσέρβα	*mia conserva*	tin
μία φέτα	*mia feta*	slice
ένα κομμάτι	*ena komati*	piece
αρκετό -α	*arketo -a*	enough
πάρα πολύ	*para poli*	too much
τίποτ' άλλο;	*tipot' alo*	anything else?
αυτά	*afta*	that's it/that's all
μία σακκούλα	*mia sakoola*	a plastic carrier bag

Notice that after a quantity word like **κιλό**/*kilo*, **λίτρο**/*litro*, **πακέτο**/*paketo*, the item or items are always in the nominative case, singular or plural. See topic vocabulary page 97 for names of food, fruit, vegetable, meat and food shops.

4 SHOPPING

AT THE CHEMIST

▶▶▶ There are many pharmacies in
Greece – recognisable by the sign:

and the lettering: **ΦΑΡΜΑΚΕΙΟ**

The *Athens News,* a daily (except Monday) paper in English, has a
list of pharmacies that are open on a rota system, if you need items at
the weekend or during the night.

The pharmacist/owner is always qualified, and is able to give
advice, take blood pressure, give injections, if necessary. On islands
and in resorts, your two most important purchases will be effective
sun tan lotion, and protection from mosquitoes. For the latter, buy a
Σπιρα-μάτ/*Spira-Mat* burner, plus tablets that are changed daily.

Με πονάει η πλάτη μου/My back hurts

Peter got too much sun yesterday and needs a few things from the
chemist. It's just possible he has a hang-over too!

Assistant:	Ορίστε, τι θέλετε; *oriste. ti thelete?*
Peter:	**Με πονάει η πλάτη μου απο τον ήλιο.** *me ponai i plati moo apo ton ilio.*
Assistant:	Αυτή η κρέμα είναι πολύ καλή. Βάλτε την τρεις φορές την ημέρα. *afti i krema ine poli kali. valte tin tris fores tin imera.*
Peter:	Ευχαριστώ. Πόσο είναι; *efharisto. posso ine?*
Assistant:	Μόνο τριακόσιες πενήντα δραχμές. **Τίποτ' άλλο;** *mono triakoses peninda thrahmes. tipot' alo?*
Peter:	Τι έχετε για κουνούπια; *ti ehete ya koonoopia?*
Assistant:	Δοκιμάστε αυτό το σπρέϊ. Έχουμε και το 'σπίρα ματ'. *thokimaste afto to sprei. Ehoome ke to' spira mat'.*
Peter:	Εντάξει. Θα πάρω το σπρέϊ. **Μου δίνετε και ένα κουτί** **ασπιρίνες και ένα αντηλιακό λάδι.** *endaksi. tha paro to sprei. moo thinete ke ena kooti* *aspirines ke ena andiliako lathi.*

4 SHOPPING

Assistant: Μάλιστα. Όλα μαζί κάνουν δύο χιλιάδες τριακόσιες
δραχμές.
malista. ola mazi kanoun dio hiliathes triakosies thrahmes.

Peter: **Πιο αργά, παρακαλώ.** Ο πονοκέφαλός μου κάνει τα
Pio arga, parakalo. O ponokefalos moo kani ta
Ελληνικά πιο δύσκολα.
ellinika pio thiskola.

Phrases from the dialogue

Με πονάει η πλάτη μου	*me ponai i plati moo*	my back hurts
απο τον ήλιο	*apo ton ilio*	from the sun
βάλτε την	*valte tin*	put it (on)
τρεις φορές την ημέρα	*tris fores tin imera*	3 times a day
για κουνούπια	*ya koonoopia*	for mosquitoes
ένα κουτί ασπιρίνες	*ena kooti aspirines*	packet of aspirin
ένα αντηλιακό λάδι	*ena andiliako lathi*	suntan oil
ένα σπρέυ	*ena sprei*	a spray
ο πονοκέφαλος	*o ponokefalos*	headache

Other useful words and phrases

Διανυκτερεύον φαρμακείο	*thianikterevon farmakio*	all night chemist
το κρυολόγημα	*to krioloyima*	cold
ο βήχας	*o vihas*	cough
το αλλεργικό συνάχι	*to aleryiko sinahi*	hay fever
το έγκαυμα του ηλίου	*to engavma too ilioo*	sunburn
η ναυτία	*i naftia*	travel sickness
η διάρροια	*i thiaria*	diarrhoea
η συνταγή	*i sindayi*	prescription

Μπορώ να το πάρω χωρις συνταγή;
boro na to paro horis sindayi
Can I take it without a
prescription?

Μπορείτε να μου ετοιμάσετε αυτή τη συνταγή;
borite na moo estimasete afti ti sindayi?
Can you make up this
prescription?

Πότε θα είναι έτοιμη;
pote tha ine etimi
When will it be ready?

4 SHOPPING

the way it works

I like/I don't like

As you saw in the first dialogue, to say you like something, you use the phrase **μ'αρέσει**/*m'aresi* in Greek.

Notice that the thing or things you like are in the nominative case, as it/they are the subject of the sentence. The person doing the liking is in the accusative (literally: 'it pleases me').

singular

μ'αρέσει ο/η/το	*m'aresi o/i/to*	I like
σ'αρέσει	*s'aresi*	you like
του/της αρέσει	*too/tis aresi*	he/she likes
μας αρέσει	*mas aresi*	we like
σας αρέσει	*sas aresi*	you like
τους αρέσει	*toos aresi*	they like

plural

μ'αρέσουν(ε) οι/οι/τα	*m'aresoon(e) i/i/ta*	I like
σ'αρέσουν(ε)	*s'aresoon(e)*	you like
του/της αρέσουν(ε)	*too/tis aresoon(e)*	he/she likes
μας αρέσουν(ε)	*mas aresoon(e)*	we like
σας αρέσουν(ε)	*sas aresoon(e)*	you like
τους αρέσουν(ε)	*toos aresoon(e)*	they like

Some examples:

Μ'αρέσει πολύ η ελληνική μουσική I like Greek music very much
m'aresi poli i eliniki moosiki
Σ'αρέσουν οι ντολμάδες; Do you like dolmathes (stuffed vine
s'aresoon i dolmathes? leaves)?
Δεν μας αρέσει το ούζο We don't like ouzo. (They don't
then mas aresi to oozo know what they're missing!)

To make this expression negative – I don't like – simply put the word **δεν**/*then* in front, e.g. **δεν μ'αρέσει**/*then m'aresi*.

Comparatives

When you want to say that something is for example cheaper or smaller than something else in Greek, there is one easy way to do it.

The word **πιο**/*pyo* before an adjective means 'more' – for example

Αυτά τα παπούτσια είναι πιο φτηνά These shoes are cheaper.
afta ta papootsia ine pio ftina.

4 SHOPPING

Το αυτοκίνητό μου είναι πιο μεγάλο.   My car is bigger.
to aftokinito moo ine pio megalo.

things to do

4.1 **At the chemist**   Match these articles with the prices in the price list opposite:

1 soap 300 dr   a δύο χιλιάδες τριακόσιες εβδομήντα πέντε δρχ

2 toothpaste 659 dr   b πεντακόσιες ενενήντα δρχ

3 sun oil 2375 dr   c τριακόσιες δρχ

4 aspirins 590 dr   d εξακόσιες πενήντα εννέα δρχ

4.2 Practice asking for the quantities of these items:

1 a kilo of apples
2 two tins of tomato juice
3 a packet of sugar
4 a litre of water

4.3 Say what you like/don't like:

1 I don't like octopus
2 I like grapes very much
3 I like Greek cheese
4 I don't like Greek cigarettes

4 SHOPPING

BUYING CLOTHES

Μπορώ να τις δοκιμάσω;/Can I try them on?

Peter needs to get a few extra clothes and heads for the shops.

Peter: **Χρειάζομαι μερικές**
hriazome merikes
μακώ μπλούζες.
mako bloozes.

Assistant: **Τι χρώμα θέλετε;**
ti hroma thelete?

Peter: **Θα ήθελα μια μπλέ**
tha ithela mia ble
και μια κίτρινη.
ke mia kitrini.

Assistant: **Τι μέγεθος είστε;**
ti megethos iste?

Peter: **Στην Αγγλία είμαι μέγεθος σαράντα, αλλά εδώ δεν ξέρω τι**
stin aglia ime megethos saranda ala etho then ksero ti
μέγεθος είμαι. Μπορώ να τις δοκιμάσω;
megethos ime. boro na tis thokimaso?

Assistant: Βεβαίως. Περάστε στο δοκιμαστήριο.
veveos. peraste sto thokimastirio.

Peter: **Η μπλέ είναι πολύ στενή. Έχετε μια πιο μεγάλη;**
i ble ine poli steni. ehete mia pio megali?

Assistant: Να κοιτάξω. Η κίτρινη σας έρχεται καλά;
na kitakso. i kitrini sas erhete kala?

Peter: Ναι. Νομίζω η κίτρινη είναι εντάξει. Ευχαριστώ. **Παίρνετε**
ne. nomizo i kitrini ine endaksi. Efharisto! Pernete
Access;
Access?

Words and phrases from the dialogue

Χρειάζομαι	*hriazome*	I need
μακώ μπλούζα -ες	*mako blooza -es*	tee shirt -s
τι χρώμα;	*ti hroma*	what colour?
τι μέγεθος είστε;	*ti megethos iste*	what size are you?
Μπορώ να τις δοκιμάσω;	*boro na tis thokimaso*	can I try them on?
Περάστε στο	*peraste sto*	go through/pass to the
δοκιμαστήριο	*thokimastirio*	fitting room
στενός -η -ο	*stenos -i -o*	tight
πιο μεγάλος -η -ο	*pio megalos -i -o*	bigger
να κοιτάξω	*na kitakso*	I'll have a look
σας έρχεται καλά	*sas erhete kala*	suits you well
στο μέγεθό σας	*sto megetho sas*	in your size
Παίρνετε Access;	*pernete Access;*	do you take Access?

4 SHOPPING

Colours

κόκκινος -η -ο	*kokinos -i -o*	red	**άσπρος -η -ο**	*aspros -i -o*	white
κίτρινος -η -ο	*kitrinos -i -o*	yellow	**μαύρος -η -ο**	*mavros -i -o*	black
πράσινος -η -ο	*prasinos -i -o*	green	**μπλέ**	*ble*	blue

Other useful words and phrases

Απλώς κοιτάω	*aplos kitao*	I'm just looking
τι χρώματα έχετε;	*ti hromata ehete*	What colours do you have?
σκούρο/ανοιχτό	*scooro/anihto*	dark/light
Τι ύφασμα είναι;	*ti ifasma ine*	What material is it?
μία μπλούζα βαμβακερή	*mia blooza vamvakeri*	cotton blouse
πάρτε μου μέτρα	*parte moo metra*	Measure me
Που είναι ο καθρέφτης;	*poo ine o kathreftis*	Where is the mirror?
Δεν μου πάει καλά	*then moo pai kala*	It doesn't suit me
Δεν μου κάνει	*then moo kani*	It doesn't fit me
Είναι πολύ κοντό	*ine poli kondo*	It's too short
μακρύ	*makri*	long
φαρδύ	*farthi*	loose
Έχετε το ίδιο σε	*ehete to ithio se*	Do you have the same in …?
Ένα ζευγάρι παπούτσια	*ena zevgari papootsia*	pair of shoes
Θα προτιμούσα	*tha protimoosa*	I'd rather have/prefer
εκπτώσεις	*ekptosis*	sales
η τιμή	*i timi*	price
Μου κάνετε μια έκπτωση;	*moo kanete mia ekptosi*	Can you give me a reduction?

See topic vocabulary for items of clothing, colours, etc.

Sizes for clothing and shoes

Shoes are a good buy in Greece, but it should be noted that the fit may be a little more generous in Greek sizes than the equivalent size in the UK.

Dresses							
UK	8	10	12	14	16	18	20
Greece	40	42	44	46	48	50	52
Suits/jackets/coats							
UK	36	38	40	42	44	46	
Greece	46	48	50	52	54	56	
Collar							
UK	13	13½	14	14½	15	15½	16	16½
Greece	33	34	35	37	38	39	41	42
Shoes							
UK	3	4	5	6	7	8	9	10
Greece	46	37	38	39/40	41	42	43	44

4 SHOPPING

▶ ▶ ▶

BUYING NEWSPAPERS

The kiosk (περίπτερο/periptero) in Greece is a vital part of everyday life, where you can make phone calls, buy newspapers and magazines, and get virtually all those little essentials you run out of late at night! Go there for postcards, sweets, matches, cigarettes, sunglasses – the list is endless.

Μου δίνετε και την Athens News;
Give me the Athens News as well

Anne and Yiannis Vazakas are walking in Syntagma Square – Anne decides to buy an English newspaper.

Anne: **Θα ήθελα να μάθω τα νέα της Αγγλίας. Που μπορώ να βρω**
tha ithela na matho ta nea tis Anglias. Poo boro na vro
αγγλικές εφημερίδες;
anglikes efimerithes?

Yiannis: Είναι πολύ εύκολο. Υπάρχουν παντού περίπτερα, που μπορείς
Ine poli efkolo. iparhoon pandoo periptera, poo boris
να αγοράσεις ό,τι θέλεις.
na agorasis oti thelis.

Anne: Θα ήθελα την εφημερίδα 'Guardian'. Την έχετε;
(going up to a kiosk) tha ithela tin efimeritha 'Guardian'.
Tin ehete?

Kiosk: Λυπάμαι, όχι, αλλά κοιτάξτε στο πλάϊ. Πρέπει να είναι εκεί
lipame, ohi, ala kitakste sto plai. prepi na ine eki
οι 'Times' και η 'Daily Mail'.
i Times ke i Daily Mail.

Anne: Α, ναι, εδώ είναι οι 'Times'.
a ne etho ine i Times.

Yiannis: Ξέρεις, Ανν, στην Ελλάδα υπάρχει η εφημερίδα 'Athens News'
στα αγγλικά.
kseris, Anne, stin Elatha iparhi i efimeritha 'Athens News'
sta anglika.

Anne: Μου δίνετε και την Athens News;
(to kiosk owner) moo thinete ke tin Athens News.

AthensNews

| TOURISTS |
Change your foreign currency at any of the 500 branches of the NATIONAL BANK the largest bank in Greece, with 55 branches around the world

LEKKA, 23-25, SYNTAGMA

| Thirty Seventh Year No. 9121 | TUESDAY, AUGUST 30, 1988 | Price Sixty drachmas (60 drs.) |

4 SHOPPING

Phrases from the dialogue

Θα ήθελα	*tha ithela*	I'd like
να μάθω	*na matho*	to learn
που μπορώ να βρώ	*poo boro na vro*	Where can I find …?
η εφημερίδα	*i efimeritha*	newspaper
εύκολο	*efkolo*	easy
παντού	*pandoo*	everywhere
που μπορείς να αγοράσεις	*poo boris na agorasis*	where you can buy
ό,τι θέλεις	*oti thelis*	whatever you like
λυπάμαι	*lipame*	I'm sorry
κοιτάξτε	*kitakste*	look (imperative)
πρέπει να είναι	*prepi na ine*	it must be
στο πλάϊ	*sto plai*	at the side

Kiosk items

πούρο (n.)	*pouro*	cigar
πακέττο τσιγάρα (n.)	*paketo tsigara*	cigarettes, packet of
σοκολάτα (f.)	*sokolata*	chocolate bar
φίλμ: φωτογραφίες (n.)	*film: fotografies*	film: prints
σλάϊντς	*slides*	slides
είκοσι τέσσερις	*ikosi teseris*	24 (exposures)
τριάντα έξι	*trianda eksi*	36 (exposures)
οδηγός (m.)	*othigos*	guide book
αναπτήρας (m.)	*anaptiras*	lighter
χάρτης (m.)	*hartis*	map
περιοδικό (n.)	*periothiko*	magazine
κουτί σπίρτα (n.)	*kouti spirta*	matches, box of
Αγγλική εφημερίδα (f.)	*angliki efimeritha*	newspaper (English)
κάρτα (f.)	*karta*	post card
στυλό (n.)	*stilo*	pen/biro
γυαλιά ηλίου (n.)	*yalia iliou*	sun glasses
καραμέλλες (f.)	*karamelles*	sweets

the way it works

How to say 'I need'

So far you've met groups of verbs ending in **-ω**/-*o*, e.g. **θέλω**/th*elo* and
-άω/-*ao*, e.g. **μιλάω**/*milao*.

At the beginning of the third dialogue, Peter uses the verb
χρειάζομαι/*hriazome*, I need. This verb belongs to another group of Greek
verbs ending in **-ομαι**/-*ome*. This is how it conjugates:

χρειάζομαι	*hriazome*	I need
χρειάζεσαι	*hriazese*	you need (sing.)
χρειάζεται	*hriazete*	he/she needs
χρειαζόμαστε	*hriazomaste*	we need
χρειάζεστε	*hriazeste*	you need (plural)
χρειάζονται	*hriazonde*	they need

4 SHOPPING

I can, I must

As you saw in the last unit, **Θέλω να**/th*elo na*, I want, is usually followed by a different form of the verb. There are two other important verbs in Greek that have the same construction, **Μπορώ να**/*boro na*, I can, and **Πρέπει να**/*prepi na*, I must. Here is the conjugation for **μπορώ**/*boro*:

Μπορώ να φύγω	*boro na figo*	I can leave
Μπορείς να φύγεις	*boris na fiyis*	you can leave
Μπορεί να φύγει	*bori na fiyi*	he can leave
Μπορούμε να φύγουμε	*boroome na figoome*	we can leave
Μπορείτε να φύγετε	*borite na fiyete*	you can leave
Μπορούν(ε) να φύγουν	*boroon(e) na figoon*	they can leave

Notice how *both* verbs change their endings.

Πρέπει να/*prepi na*, I must, however, is an impersonal verb and stays the same in all persons. Only the verb that follows changes its endings:

Πρέπει να πάω	*prepi na pao*	I must go
Πρέπει να πας	*prepi na pas*	you must go
Πρέπει να πάει	*prepi na pai*	he must go
Πρέπει να πάμε	*prepi na pame*	we must go
Πρέπει να πάτε	*prepi na pate*	you must go
Πρέπει να πάνε	*prepi na pane*	they must go

See page 66 for the future forms of other common verbs which are used after **μπορώ να**/*boro na* and **πρέπει να**/*prepi na*.

things to do

4.4 Complete this dialogue in a shoe shop

You:	(Do you have these shoes in my size?)
Assistant:	**Τι μέγεθος είστε, κυρία;**
	ti megethos iste, kiria?
You:	(In England I'm size 6. What's that in Greece?)
Assistant:	**Είναι τριάντα εννέα.**
	ine trianda ennea.
You:	(I like the blue ones)
Assistant:	**Τα μπλέ, μέγεθος τριάντα εννέα – Ένα λεπτό, κυρία.**
	ta ble, megethos 39 – ena lepto, kiria.
You:	(they are a little large – can I try size 38?)
Assistant:	**Λυπάμαι, δεν έχουμε. Τα έχω σε καφέ.**
	lipame, then ehoume. Ta eho se kafe.
You:	(OK, I'll take the brown, size 38)

4.5 Ask where/if you can do the following:

1 Can I see the menu, please?
2 Can we have a table for four, please?
3 Where can I find a chemist?
4 Can I try on this dress, please?

5 SIGHTSEEING AND LEISURE

EXCURSIONS

Sea travel Pireus is the main port of Athens. Ships leave from there for the islands in the Saronic and Aegean. The hydrofoils (**Το ιπτάμενο**/*iptameno*), or Flying Dolphins, offer a fast service to the near islands of Aegina, Poros, Hydra, Spetses for example, and leave from their own moorings at Marina Zea in Pireus. You can also go by Flying Dolphin to the islands of the Sporades, Skiathos, Skopelos and Alonisos – leaving from Agios Konstantinos and Volos. Hydrofoil tickets should be booked in advance during the peak tourist season from the office in Syntagma Square, or through travel agents.

Με το πλοίο για τη Μύκονο
By boat to Mikonos

Peter, Maria and Costas decide to take a boat trip to another island to get a change of scenery.

Peter: **Πόση ώρα κάνει το πλοίο για τη Μύκονο;**
            posi ora kani to plio ya ti Mikono?

Costas: Τρεις ώρες περίπου.
            tris ores peripoo.

Peter: **Σταματάει σε άλλα νησιά;**
            stamatai se alla nisia?

Costas: Στη Δήλο, για μια ώρα. **Πρέπει να αγοράσουμε τα εισιτήρια**
            stin Delo, ya mi ora. prepi na agorassoome ta isitiria
            αμέσως, γιατί έχει πάντα πολύ κόσμο.
            amesos, yati ehi panda poli kosmo.

5 SIGHTSEEING AND LEISURE

Maria: Τι θέση θα ταξιδέψουμε;
ti thesi tha taksithepsoome?

Costas: **Τουριστική γιατί είναι πιο φτηνή.**
tooristiki yati ine pyo ftini.

Peter: **Τι καιρό θα έχουμε;**
ti kero tha ehoome?

Maria: Θα έχουμε λίγο θάλασσα. **Μήπως παθαίνεις ναυτία,** Peter;
tha ehoome ligo thalasa. mipos pathenis naftia, Peter?

Peter: Μέχρι τώρα όχι, αλλά δεν ταξιδεύω με πλοίο συχνά.
mehri tora ohi, alla then taksithevo me plio sihna.

Words and phrases from the dialogue

Πόση ώρα κάνει το πλοίο;	*posi ora kani to plio?*	How long does the boat take?
περίπου	*peripoo*	about
σταματάει;	*stamatai?*	does it stop?
σε άλλα νησιά	*se alla nisia*	at other islands
πρέπει να -ουμε ...	*prepi na -oome ...*	we must ...
αμέσως	*amesos*	straight away
γιατί	*yati*	because
πολύς κόσμος	*polis kosmos*	a lot of people
πάντα	*panda*	always
Τι θέση;	*ti thesi*	what seats (i.e. what class)?
Θα ταξιδέψουμε;	*tha taksithepsoome?*	shall we travel?
Τι καιρό θα έχουμε;	*ti kero tha ehoome?*	what weather will we have?
μήπως	*mipos*	perhaps
παθαίνω ναυτία	*patheno naftia*	I suffer from seasickness
μέχρι τώρα	*mehri tora*	until now
με πλοίο	*me plio*	by boat
συχνά	*sihna*	all the time/continuously

Other useful words and phrases

Που βγάζουνε εισιτήρια;	*poo vgazoone isitiria?*	where do they issue tickets?
το πρακτορείο	*to praktorio*	ticket office/agency
Πληροφορίες	*plirofories*	information
το ταξίδι	*to taksithi*	journey
το φέρρυ-μποτ	*to feri bot*	car ferry
η καμπίνα	*i kabina*	cabin
Πρώτη θέση	*proti thesi*	first class seats
το κατάστρωμα	*to katastroma*	deck
το λιμάνι	*to limani*	harbour
η παραλία	*i paralia*	coast/seashore

Με το πούλμαν για τους Δελφούς
By coach to Delphi

Anne has agreed to meet Mr and Mrs Vazakas, and go with them on a day trip to Delphi – the site of the ancient oracle – by coach.

Yiannis: Να η Anne. Έρχεται!
na i Anne. erhete!

Eleni: Γειά σου Anne. Είσαι στην ώρα σου όπως όλοι οι Άγγλοι.
yasoo Anne. ise stin ora soo opos oli i angli.

Anne: Γειά σας. **Τι ωραίος καιρός σήμερα!**
yasas. ti oreos keros simera!

Yiannis: Το λεωφορείο φεύγει στις οκτώμιση και φτάνει στους
to leoforio fevyi stis oktomisi ke ftani stoos
Δελφούς στις εντεκάμιση.
thelfous stis endekamisi.

Anne: **Ωραία. Τι θα δούμε στους Δελφούς;**
orea. ti tha thoome stoos thelfoos?

Yiannis: Θα δούμε το Μουσείο, το Στάδιο και το Μαντείο.
tha thoome to moosioo, to stathio ke to mandio.

Anne: Πόσες ώρες θα μείνουμε εκεί;
poses ores tha menoome eki?

Eleni: Τέσσερις-πέντε. Το βράδυ θα έρθεις στο σπίτι μας
teseris pende to vrathi tha erthis sto spiti mas
να φάμε μαζί.
na fame mazi.

Anne: Ευχαριστώ πολύ. Η ελληνική φιλοξενία είναι φημισμένη
παντού!
efharisto poli. i eliniki filoksenia ine fimismeni pandoo!

5 SIGHTSEEING AND LEISURE

Words and phrases from the dialogue

η Ανν έρχεται	i Anne erhete	Anne is coming
στην ώρα	stin ora	on time
όπως όλοι οι Άγγλοι	opos oli i Angli	like all the English
Τι ωραίος καιρός!	ti oreos keros!	what lovely weather!
σήμερα	simera	today
στους Δελφούς	stoos thelfoos	at Delphi
Τι θα δούμε;	ti tha thoome	what will we see?
το στάδιο	to stathio	stadium
το Μαντείο	to Mandio	Oracle
θα μείνουμε	tha menoome	will we stay
το βράδυ	to vrathi	in the evening
θα έρθεις στο σπίτι μας	tha erthis sto spiti mas	you'll come to our house
να φάμε μαζί	na fame mazi	for us to eat together
η φιλοξενία	i filoksenia	hospitality
φημισμένος -η -ο	fimismenos -i -o	famous
παντού	pandoo	everywhere

Other useful words and phrases

με το πούλμαν	me to poolman	by coach
η εκδρομή	i ekthromi	trip/excursion
ο συνοδός	o sinothos	courier
ο ξεναγός	o ksenagos	guide
ο οδηγός	o othigos	driver
αποσκευές	aposkeves	luggage
αυτή είναι η θέση μου	afti ine i thesi moo	this is my seat
που θα σταματήσουμε;	poo tha stamatisoome?	where will we stop?

Vocabulary of Ancient Greece

η αγορά	i agora	ancient market place
το αμφιθέατρο	to amfitheatro	amphitheatre
ο ναός	o naos	temple
η κολώνα	i kolona	column
τα ερείπια	ta eripia	ruins

5 SIGHTSEEING AND LEISURE

Καλώς ώρισες στο σπίτι μας
Welcome to our house

Anne and her Greek friends have had a wonderful day out, and have now returned to the Vazakas' house in Pagrati.

Eleni: **Καλώς ώρισες στο σπίτι μας**, Anne.
kalos orises sto spiti mas, Anne.

Anne: **Καλώς σας βρήκα!** Κάτι τέτοιο λέτε, έτσι δεν είναι;
kalos sas vrika. kati tetio lete, etsi then ine?

Yiannis: Anne, έγινες πραγματική Ελληνίδα. Πέρασε στη βεράντα –
Anne, eyines pragmatiki elinitha. perase sti veranda –
Τι θα πάρεις;
ti tha paris?

Anne: Λίγο κρασί άσπρο με σόδα, ευχαριστώ.
ligo krasi aspro me sotha, efharisto.

Yiannis: **Πως περνάς στις διακοπές;**
pos pernas stis thiakopes?

Anne: **Περνάω πολύ ωραία. Διασκεδάζω πολύ. Ευχαριστώ πολύ για**
pernao poli orea. thiaskethazo poli. efharisto poli ya
την πρόσκληση. Το σπίτι σας είναι θαυμάσιο. Μένετε εδώ
tin prosklisi. to spiti sas ine thavmasio. menete etho
πολύ καιρό;
poli kero?

Eleni: Μένουμε εδώ δέκα χρόνια. Είναι πολύ κοντά στο κέντρο και
menoome etho theka hronya. ine poli konda sto kendro ke
βλέπουμε την
vlepoome tin
Ακρόπολη.
Akropoli.

Anne: **Τι όμορφη θέα!**
ti omorfi thea!

Yiannis: Τι θα κάνεις το
ti tha kanis to
Σαββατοκύριακο;
savatokiriako?
Πάμε στα μπουζούκια;
pame sta boozookia?

Words and phrases from the dialogue

καλώς ωρίσατε	*kalos orisate*	welcome
καλώς σας βρήκα	*kalos sas vrika*	I'm glad to be here
		(= I've found you well)
κάτι τέτοιο λέτε	*kati tetio lete*	you say something like that
έτσι δεν είναι;	*etsi then ine*	isn't it?/don't you?, etc.
έγινες	*eyines*	you've become
πέρασε	*perase*	pass through (imperative)
τι θα πάρεις;	*ti tha paris?*	what will you have/drink?
πως περνάς;	*pos pernas*	how are you spending your time?

στις διακοπές	stis diakopes	on holiday
περνάω πολύ ωραία	pernao poli orea	I'm having a good time
διασκεδάζω	thiaskethazo	I'm enjoying myself
η πρόσκληση	i prosklisi	invitation
θαυμάσιος -α -ο	thavmasios -a -o	wonderful
πολύ καιρό	poli kero	a long time
βλέπουμε	vlepoome	we see/we can see
Τι όμορφη θέα	ti omorfi thea	what a beautiful view!
το Σαββατοκύριακο	to savatokiriako	the weekend
στα μπουζούκια	sta boozookia	to a bouzouki place

Other useful words and phrases

το διαμέρισμα	to thiamerisma	flat/apartment
το μπαλκόνι	to balkoni	balcony
πως είναι το σπίτι;	pos ine to spiti	what's your house like?
που μένετε;	poo menete?	where do you live?
καθίστε	kathiste	sit down/take a seat
καπνίζετε;	kapnizete?	do you smoke?
(δεν) καπνίζω	(then) kapnizo	I (don't) smoke

the way it works

Future tense

To form the future (e.g. I'll go), put the word **θα**/tha before the verb. There are some verbs which keep their normal present tense form after **θα**/tha – e.g. **κάνω**/kano: **θα κάνω**/tha kano (I'll do/make); **περιμένω**/perimeno; **θα περιμένω**/tha perimeno (I'll wait).

Most verbs, however, change their form after **θα**/tha. Here are the most important:

Present		Future		
πηγαίνω	piyeno	Θα πάω	tha pao	I'll go
στέλνω	stelno	Θα στείλω	tha stilo	I'll send
παίρνω	perno	Θα πάρω	tha paro	I'll take
μένω	meno	Θα μείνω	tha mino	I'll stay
αγοράζω	agorazo	Θα αγοράσω	tha agoraso	I'll buy
τηλεφωνώ	tilefono	Θα τηλεφωνήσω	tha tilefonisso	I'll phone
νοικιάζω	nikiazo	Θα νοικιάσω	tha nikiaso	I'll hire
χαλάω	halao	Θα χαλάσω	tha halasso	I'll change
λέω	leo	Θα πω	tha po	I'll say
βλέπω	vlepo	Θα δω	tha tho	I'll see

Some examples:

Θα πάμε στην Ελλάδα του χρόνου.
tha pame stin elatha too hronoo
We'll go to Greece next year

Η Μαρία θα στείλει μια κάρτα στη μητέρα της
i Maria tha stili mia karta sti mitera tis
Maria will send a postcard to her mother

5 SIGHTSEEING AND LEISURE

Orders and Instructions (con)

On Wednesday you met the plural/polite imperative form.

In the last dialogue Yiannis asks Anne to pass through to the veranda. As he knows her quite well now, he uses **πέρασε**/*perase*, which is the singular/familiar form of the imperative. Here is a list of common verbs, showing the form.

First person present		*Familiar imperative*		
φέρνω	*ferno*	**φέρε**	*fere*	bring
πηγαίνω	*piyeno*	**πήγαινε**	*piyene*	go
δίνω	*thino*	**δώσε**	*those*	give
έρχομαι	*erhome*	**έλα**	*ela*	come
κάθομαι	*kathome*	**κάτσε**	*katse*	sit
παίρνω	*perno*	**πάρε**	*pare*	take
περιμένω	*perimeno*	**περίμενε**	*perimene*	wait
αφήνω	*afino*	**άσε**	*ase*	leave
λέω	*leo*	**πες**	*pes*	say
στρίβω	*strivo*	**στρίψε**	*stripse*	turn
περνάω	*pernao*	**πέρασε**	*perase*	pass
δοκιμάζω	*thokimazo*	**δοκίμασε**	*thokimase*	try

things to do

.1 The details of your excursion haven't been announced yet, so:

1 Ask what time the boat leaves
2 Ask how much the ticket is
3 Ask how long the trip lasts
4 Ask when the boat returns
5 Ask where you'll have lunch
6 Ask if you must buy tickets now

.2 You've found a seat next to a Greek person on a bus. Complete the dialogue:

You: (Ask if the seat is free)
Greek: **Ναι – καθίστε. Πηγαίνετε στη Βουλιαγμένη;**
You: (Say no – you have to get off at Glyfada)
Greek: **Ξέρετε που πρέπει να κατεβείτε;**
You: (No, you're not sure – ask if he/she can tell you where)
Greek: **Ασφαλώς – Είστε εδώ για διακοπές;**
You: (Yes, but you'll be leaving in two days)

5 ENTERTAINMENT

AN EVENING OUT

With such wonderful sea, landscape, food, drink and people, all life is entertainment in Greece!

Greeks like to eat out in the evenings, usually well after 9.00 pm and go on into the small hours. Discos and cocktail bars are plentiful and fashionable on the islands – in Athens you'll need to ask your hotel to recommend night clubs and discos to suit your taste and pocket.

In the summer months cinemas are in the open air. Most films are imported and always shown with their original soundtrack and Greek subtitles – so you won't miss out on new releases.

For a traditional Greek evening out, you can go to a bouzouki place, where you'll hear traditional Greek songs accompanied by the mandolin-like bouzouki, which gives Greek music its distinctive sound, and often Greek dancing. You probably won't see any plates being smashed now, by the way. Bouzouki places can be quite expensive, so check first – you may also have to book ahead. Remember, things get going quite late, so don't turn up at 7.00 pm!

In Athens you can attend classical music concerts at the Herod Atticus Theatre at the foot of the Acropolis. See the publication *The Athenian* for weekly events, or a copy of *Athens News* (daily except Mondays), an English language newspaper available from central kiosks in Athens. This gives details of all events, concerts and films.

5 ENTERTAINMENT

Θέλω τρία εισιτήρια για αύριο
Three tickets for tomorrow, please

Anne wants some tickets for a play.

Anne: **Θέλω τρία εισιτήρια για αύριο. Πρέπει να τα κλείσω τώρα, ή**
thelo tria isitiria ya avrio. Prepi na ta kliso tora, i
μπορώ να τα αγοράσω πριν την παράσταση;
boro na ta agorasso prin tin parastasi?

Clerk: Θα έχει πολύ κόσμο. Πρέπει να κλείσετε τις θέσεις τώρα.
tha ehi poli kosmo. prepi na klisete tis thesis tora.

Anne: Εντάξει. **Θέλω τρεις θέσεις στην πλατεία για τη βραδινή**
endaksi. thelo tris thesis stin platia ya tin vrathini
παράσταση. Τι ώρα αρχίζει;
parastasi. Ti ora arhizi?

Clerk: Στις εννιά. Λοιπόν, έχω τρεις πολύ καλές θέσεις στην τρίτη
stis enya. lipon, eho tris poli kales thesis stin triti
σειρά. Κοστίζουν οκτακόσιες δραχμές η κάθε μία. Δύο
sira. Kostizoon aktakosies thrahmes i kathe mia. Thio
χιλιάδες τετρακόσιες δραχμές.
hiliathes tetrakosies thrahmes.

Anne: **Ευχαριστώ για τη βοήθεια.**
efharisto ya ti voithia.

ΘΕΑΤΡΑ

AΘHNA (Πατησίων και Δεριγνύ, τηλ 8237330) Λουι Βερνέιγ «Κρατικές υποθέσεις»· Β. Βουλγαρίδης Β' Πάλλης Μπ. Λσημακοπούλου κ.ά.

AΘHNAION (Πατησίων 55, τηλ 8214000, 8233048) «Λίγο πιο νωρίς, λίγο πιο αργά» των Μπαριγέ και Γκρεντί · Βουγιουκλάκη, Λαμπροπούλου, Μουτούσης, Σπυρόπουλος

AKPOAMA (Ιουλιανού 35 και 3ης Σεπτεμβρίου 78, τηλ. 8232 8691 «Εγώ, αυτές και τα μυστήρια» των Καμπανή, Μακρίδη Ν. Παπαναστασίου. Τ. Σχοινάκη, Ν. Βερβέλης

BEAKEIO Μικρή Πόρτα· «Το ημέρωμα της Στρίγκλας» του Σαίξπηρ ΔΗΠΕΘΕ Ιωαννίνων (Τρίτη)· «Αγαμέμνων» του Αισχύλου από το Αμφιθέατρο του Σπ Ευαγγελάτου (Σαββάτο) Τις υπόλοιπες μέρες αργεί

ΛAMΠETH (Λεωφ. Αλεξάνδρας 106, τηλ. 5463685) «Πονηρό πνεύμα» του Νοελ Κάουαρντ · Κ. Καρράς, Ν. Βαλσάμη, Π. Ζούνη, Θ. Μπαζάκα

ΛOYZITANIA (Ευελπίδων 47, Πεδίον Αρεως, τηλ. 8827201) Ν. Αθερινού · Στ Φιλιππούλη · Α. Στεφανοπούλου «Μη μασάς τη αφραρίτα»· Γ. Γκιωνάκης, Σ. Τζιβελέκος, Λ. Μελίντα Ο. Πολίτου

ΛYKABHTTOΣ (7227209). Συνωλιά Μάριου Τόκα

METPOΠOΛITAN (Λ. Αλεξάνδρας 14, τηλ. 8223 333) «Η βίδα» του Γ. Σανθούλη· Θ. Καρακατσάνης, Κ. Μπαλανίκα, κ.ά

MINΩA (Πατησίων 91. τηλ. 8210048) «Πως την κάνω τη βαζελίνη Τουρκία»· των Σ. Φιλιππίδου · Χ. Ρώμα Με τους: Κ Βουτσά Ντ Ηλιοπούλο, Γ. Μιχαλόπουλο κ.ά

Words and phrases from the dialogue

Για αύριο	*ya avrio*	for tomorrow
πρέπει να τα κλείσω;	*prepi na ta kliso*	Do I have to book them?
ή μπορώ να τα αγοράσω;	*i boro na ta agorasso*	or can I buy them …?
πριν την παράσταση	*prin tin parastasi*	before the performance
πρέπει να κλείσετε	*prepi na klisete*	you must book
τρεις θέσεις στην πλατεία	*tris thesis stin platia*	3 seats in the stalls
βραδινή παράσταση	*vrathini parastasi*	evening performance
στη τρίτη σειρά	*stin triti sira*	in the third row
για τη βοήθεια	*ya tin voithia*	for (your) help

5 ENTERTAINMENT

Other useful words and phrases

Going to the cinema or theatre

Το σινεμά	*to sinema*	cinema
το έργο/φίλμ	*to ergo/film*	film (also η ταινία/*i tenia*)
το πρόγραμμα	*to programa*	programme
Είναι το φίλμ στα Αγγλικά;	*ine to film sta anglika?*	Is the film in English?

Η απογευματινή/βραδινή παράσταση	afternoon/evening performance
i apoyevmatini/vrathini parastasi	
το διάλειμμα	interval
to thialima	
Τι παίζει στο σινεμά;	What's on (what's playing)
ti pezi sto sinema?	at the cinema?

Τι ώρα αρχίζει/τελειώνει;	*ti ora arhizi/telioni?*	What time does it start/finish?
η συναυλία	*i sinavlia*	concert
το θέατρο	*to theatro*	theatre
το έργο	*to ergo*	play
η πλατεία	*i platia*	stalls
ο εξώστης	*o eksostis*	balcony

Θέλω να κλείσω δυο εισιτήρια για	I want to book two tickets for
thelo na kliso thio isitiria ya	

το αστυνομικό	*to astinomiko*	detective (film)
η κωμωδία	*i komothia*	comedy
το δράμα	*to thrama*	drama
το μουσικοχορευτικό	*to moosikohoreftiko*	musical

Going out on the town

Πρέπει να κλείσουμε	*prepi na klisoome*	do we have to reserve
ένα τραπέζι;	*ena trapezi?*	a table?
η ντίσκο	*i disko*	discotheque
το ναϊτκλαμπ	*to naitklub*	nightclub
το κέντρο	*to kendro*	bouzouki place

Πάμε στα μπουζούκια;	*pame sta boozookia?*	shall we go to a bouzouki place?
Πάμε για χορό;	*pame ya horo?*	shall we go dancing?

Θέλω να νοικιάσω ένα ποδήλατο θάλασσας
I want to hire a pedal boat

Peter wants to hire a pedal boat for an hour or so.

Peter: **Θέλω να νοικιάσω ένα ποδήλατο θάλασσας για μια ώρα.**
thelo na nikiaso ena pothilato thalassas ya mia ora.
Πόσο κάνει;
Poso kani?

Boy: Τριακόσιες δραχμές η μια ώρα – πεντακόσιες για δύο ώρες.
Triakosies thrahmes i mia ora – pendakosies ya thio ores.

5 ENTERTAINMENT

Peter: **Νομίζω μια ώρα είναι αρκετά.**
Nomizo mia ora ine arketa.

Boy: Εντάξει. Αλλά δεν πρέπει να πάτε πέρα απο τις σημαδούρες.
Endaksi. ala then prepi na pate pera apo tis simathoores.

Peter: Μήπως υπάρχουν καρχαρίες πιο έξω;
(laughingly) *mipos iparhoon karharies pio ekso?*

Useful words and phrases from the dialogue

Θέλω να νοικιάσω	thelo na nikiaso	I want to hire
ένα ποδήλατο θάλασσας	ena pothilato thalassas	pedal boat
για μια ώρα	ya mia ora	for an hour
νομίζω	nomizo	I think
είναι αρκετά	ine arketa	is enough
δεν πρέπει να πάτε	then prepi na pate	you mustn't go
πέρα απο τις σημαδούρες	pera apo tis simathoores	beyond the buoys
καρχαρίες	karharies	sharks
πιο έξω	pio ekso	further out

Other useful words and phrases

On the beach

ΑΠΑΓΟΡΕΥΕΤΑΙ ΤΟ ΚΟΛΥΜΠΙ!   swimming prohibited
apagorevete to kolimbi

Πως είναι η πλάζ – έχει άμμο ή πέτρες;   how's the beach – sand or pebbles?
pos ine i plaz – ehi amo i petres

Είναι η θάλασσα επικίνδυνη εδώ;   is the sea dangerous here?
ine i thalasa epikinthini etho?

Υπάρχει ακτοφύλακας;	iparhi aktofilakas?	is there a lifeguard?
Υπάρχουν ρεύματα;	iparhoon revmata?	are there currents?
το στρώμα θάλασσας	to stroma thalassas	beach mat
η καμπίνα	i kabina	cabin
ο πάγκος	o pangos	lounger
η τέντα	i tenda	sunshade
η ομπρέλλα	i ombrella	parasol/umbrella
Μπορώ να νοικιάσω;	boro na nikiaso …?	Can I hire …?

Πως λέτε 'surfboard'
    στα Ελληνικά;
	Pos lete 'surfboard'
	    sta Ellinika?
		What is 'surfboard'
		    in Greek?

71

5   ENTERTAINMENT

Camping

το κάμπινγκ	*to kamping*	campsite
η κατασκήνωση	*i kataskinosi*	campsite
η σκηνή	*i skini*	tent
το τροχόσπιτο	*to trohospito*	caravan/trailer

Που μπορούμε να κατασκηνώσουμε τη νύχτα;
poo boroome na kataskinosoome ti nihta?
where can we camp for night?

Μπορούμε να ανάψουμε φωτιά;
boroome na anapsoome fotia?
can we light a fire?

Το νερό – είναι πόσιμο;
to nero – ine posimo?
is the water drinkable?

Υπάρχουν ντους/λουτρά/τουαλέττες;
iparhoon doosh/lootra/tooaletes?
are there showers/baths/toilets?

things to do

5.3 You want to buy tickets for a play:

1 Ask if there are seats for this evening
2 Ask how much the tickets are
3 Say you want four tickets
4 Ask how much that is altogether
5 Ask what time the performance starts and finishes

ΚΕΑ (Υπερείδου 21, Πλάκα, τηλ. 3229889): «Ασπρο - μαύρο», μονόπρακτα των Οσκαρ Γουάιλντ, Γκελντερόντ, Μπέλλου.

ΚΕΡΚΙΔΑ (Σοφούλη 31, θύρα 10 γηπέδου Πανιωνίου, τηλ. 9349560). «Το φιντανάκι» των Π. Χορν - Νότα Παρούση, Τάκης Σταματάτος.

ΦΛΟΡΙΝΤΑ (Μετσόβου 4 και Πατησίων, τηλ.: 8228501) Γ. Κατσαμπή: «Ενα κορίτσι στη ...μπανιέρα μου». Κ. Παπανίκα - Θ. Κατσαδράμης. κ.ά.

ΘΕΑΤΡΟ ΔΟΡΑΣ ΣΤΡΑΤΟΥ (Λόφος Φιλοππάπου): «Ελληνικοί χοροί».

5.4 You want to organise something for the evening and ask the hotel receptionist:

You:	(Ask what's on at the cinema tonight)
Receptionist:	Παίζει μία ελληνική ταινία.
You:	(Ask what else you can do)
Receptionist:	Πρέπει να πάτε στα μπουζούκια.
You:	(Ask if you have to book a table)
Receptionist:	Ναι, νομίζω. Θέλετε να τηλεφωνήσω;
You:	(Say yes – ask for a table for two at 9.30pm)

6 ON THE ROAD

TRAVELLING BY CAR OR BIKE

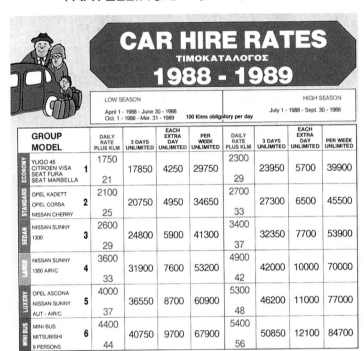

CAR HIRE RATES
ΤΙΜΟΚΑΤΑΛΟΓΟΣ
1988 - 1989

	LOW SEASON				HIGH SEASON			
	April 1 - 1988 - June 30 - 1988 Oct. 1 - 1988 - Mar. 31 - 1989		100 Klms obligatory per day		July 1 - 1988 - Sept. 30 - 1988			
GROUP MODEL	DAILY RATE PLUS KLM	3 DAYS UNLIMITED	EACH EXTRA DAY UNLIMITED	PER WEEK UNLIMITED	DAILY RATE PLUS KLM	3 DAYS UNLIMITED	EACH EXTRA DAY UNLIMITED	PER WEEK UNLIMITED
ECONOMY YUGO 45 CITROEN VISA **1** SEAT FURA SEAT MARBELLA	1750 21	17850	4250	29750	2300 29	23950	5700	39900
STANDARD OPEL KADETT OPEL CORSA **2** NISSAN CHERRY	2100 25	20750	4950	34650	2700 33	27300	6500	45500
SEDAN NISSAN SUNNY 1300 **3**	2600 29	24800	5900	41300	3400 37	32350	7700	53900
LARGE NISSAN SUNNY 1300 AIR/C **4**	3600 33	31900	7600	53200	4900 42	42000	10000	70000
LUXERY OPEL ASCONA NISSAN SUNNY **5** AUT - AIR/C	4000 37	36550	8700	60900	5300 48	46200	11000	77000
MINI BUS MINI BUS MITSUBISHI **6** 9 PERSONS	4400 44	40750	9700	67900	5400 56	50850	12100	84700

Hiring a car/motorbike Cars cost a great deal more in Greece than other European countries, so car hire is more expensive too. It's worth it, though, to get out into the countryside, or to find secluded beaches.

Most car rental agencies in Athens are situated at the top of Syngrou Avenue, opposite Hadrian's Gate. Your hotel can also arrange car hire. You'll need a current driving licence, of course, and your passport. It is advisable, although expensive, to take out full collision protection – Greeks are enthusiastic and boisterous drivers, who give no quarter to cautious drivers!

On the islands there are many small car and motorbike rental businesses. Motorbikes are convenient for getting around cheaply, especially on a bigger island, but be very careful at night on small roads – a lot of accidents happen.

6 ON THE ROAD

Θέλω να νοικιάσω ένα αυτοκίνητο
I want to hire a car

Peter, Costas and Maria want to hire a car for the day.

Costas: **Θέλω να νοικιάσω ένα αυτοκίνητο.** Το πιο μικρό που έχετε.
thelo na nikiaso ena aftokinito – to pio mikro poo ehete.

Assistant: **Τι μάρκα θέλετε;**
ti marka thelete?

Costas: Ένα Φίατ με δύο πόρτες.
ena Fiat me thio portes.

Assistant: Εντάξει. Για πόσες μέρες το θέλετε;
endaksi – ya posses meres to thelete?

Maria: Μόνο για μια μέρα.
mono ya mia mera.

Costas: **Πόσο κάνει μαζί με την ασφάλεια;**
poso kani mazi me tin asfalia?

Assistant: Τέσσερις χιλιάδες το αυτοκίνητο, χίλιες η ασφάλεια.
tesseris hiliathes to aftokinito, hilies i asfalia.
Επιπλέον, τριάντα δραχμές κατά χιλιόμετρο. Πρέπει να
epipleon, trianda thrahmes kata hiliometro, prepi na
πληρώσετε μια προκαταβολή. **Μπορώ να δω την άδεια**
plirosete mia prokatavoli. Boro na tho tin athia
οδηγήσεώς σας, παρακαλώ;
othiyeseos sas, parakalo?

Costas: Ορίστε. Ειναι καθαρή!
oriste ine kathari!

Words and phrases from the dialogue

Θέλω να νοικιάσω	*thelo na nikiaso*	I want to hire
το αυτοκίνητο	*to aftokinito*	car
το πιο μικρό	*to pio mikro*	the smallest
με δύο πόρτες	*me thio portes*	with 2 doors
η ασφάλεια	*i asfalia*	insurance
επιπλέον	*epipleon*	on top of that
κατά χιλιόμετρο	*kata hiliometro*	per kilometre
πρέπει να πληρώσετε	*prepi na plirosete*	you must pay
η προκαταβολή	*i prokatavoli*	deposit
η άδεια οδηγήσεως	*i athia othiyiseos*	driving licence
καθαρός -ή -ό	*katharos -i -o*	clean

6 ON THE ROAD

Other useful words and phrases

αυτόματο	aftomato	automatic (gears)
έχει ραδιόφωνο	ehi rathiofono	it has a radio
κασσετόφωνο	kasetofono	cassette player
Μπορώ να αφήσω το	boro na afiso to	can I leave the
αυτοκίνητο στο/στην ...	aftokinito sto/stin ...	car in ...?
Με ελεύθερα χιλιόμετρα	me elefthera hiliometra	unlimited kms
ημερήσια χρέωση	imerisia hreosi	daily charge
εβδομαδιαία χρέωση	evthomathiea hreosi	weekly charge
φόροι	fori	taxes
η παράδοση	i parathosi	delivery
η παραλαβή	i paralavi	collection
η πλήρης ασφάλεια	i pliris asfalia	full insurance

Road signs

ΑΔΙΕΞΟΔΟΣ	ATHIEKSOTHOS	NO THROUGH ROAD
ΑΠΑΓΟΡΕΥΕΤΑΙ	APAGOREVETE	
Η ΕΙΣΟΔΟΣ	I ISOTHOS	NO ENTRY
Η ΣΤΑΘΜΕΥΣΗ	I STATHMEFSI	NO PARKING
ΤΟ ΠΡΟΣΠΕΡΑΣΜΑ	TO PROSPERASMA	NO OVERTAKING
Η ΑΝΑΜΟΝΗ	I ANAMONI	NO WAITING
ΔΗΜΟΣΙΑ ΕΡΓΑ	THIMOSIA ERGA	ROAD WORKS
ΚΙΝΔΥΝΟΣ/ΠΡΟΣΟΧΗ	KINTHINOS/PROSOHI	CAUTION
ΜΟΝΟΔΡΟΜΟΣ	MONOTHROMOS	ONE WAY STREET
ΠΑΡΑΚΑΜΠΤΗΡΙΟΣ	PARAKAMPTIRIOS	DIVERSION
ΑΡΓΑ	ARGA	SLOW

Driving in Greece In Greece you drive on the right. In town the speed limit is between 40 and 60 kph; on trunk roads between 80 and 100 kph. Place names are signposted in Greek and Roman letters. The equivalent of the AA/RAC is ELPA. ELPA also has tourist information offices in larger towns.

Petrol is available in two grades – 2 star (regular) and 4 star (super). Unleaded petrol is also available.

Motoring in Greece

On the road

οδηγείτε δεξιά	othiyite theksia	drive on the right
η Εθνική οδός	i ethniki othos	motorway
τα διόδια	ta thiothia (plu.)	toll
η διασταύρωση	i thiastavrosi	junction
το φανάρι/τα φανάρια	to fanari/ta fanaria	traffic light/s
η κυκλοφορία	i kikloforia	traffic
η ταχύτητα	i tahitita	speed
το όριο ταχύτητας	to orio tahititas	speed limit
το πάρκινγκ	to parking	car park
το παρκόμετρο	to parkometro	parking meter

6 ON THE ROAD

At the petrol station

το πρατήριο Βενζίνης	to pratirio venzinis	petrol station
η βενζίνη	i venzini	petrol
απλή	apli	regular (2*)
σούπερ	sooper	super (4*)
Βάλτε μου βενζίνη για ...	valte moo venzini ya ...	give me ... drachmas
δραχμές	thrahmes	worth of petrol
Γεμίστε το	yemiste to	fill it up
το λάδι	to lathi	oil
ελέγξτε το λάδι	elengste to lathi	check the oil
τα λάστιχα	ta lastiha	tyres
η πίεση	i piesi	pressure
το ντίζελ	to dizel	diesel
το τροχόσπιτο	to trohospito	caravan

Asking the way

Πόσα χιλιόμετρα είναι μέχρι ...;
posa hiliometra ine mehri ...?
how many km is it to ...?

Μπορείτε να μου δείξετε το δρόμο για ...;
borite na moo thiksete to thromo ya ...?
can you show me the way to ...?

Που οδηγεί αυτός ο δρόμος;
poo othiyi aftos o thromos?
where does this road lead to ...?

Δείξτε μου που είμαι στο χάρτη
thikste moo poo ime sto harti
show me where I am on the map

Έχετε πάρει λάθος δρόμο
ehete pari lathos thromo
you've taken the wrong road

things to do

6.1 You want to hire a car. Fill in the missing words in Greek:

You: (I want to hire) **ένα αυτοκίνητο** (with four doors).
Car Hire: Τι μάρκα προτιμάτε;
You: **Θέλω** (a cheap car)
Car Hire: Έχω ένα Opel Corsa.
You: (How much does it cost for 1 day?)
Car Hire: Δέκα χιλιάδες δρχ τη μέρα. Για πόσες μέρες το θέλετε;
You: (for three days)
Car Hire: Μπορώ να δω την άδεια οδηγήσεως;

6.2 You stop at a petrol station:

1 Ask for a tank full of 4 star petrol
2 Ask for the oil to be checked
3 Ask if the road goes to Athens
4 Ask how many kilometres it is to Athens

6 ON THE ROAD

A CAR BREAKDOWN

Έχει μια βλάβη/We've had a breakdown

Peter, Maria and Costas are driving along the coast, looking for a place to swim. Suddenly the car stops. Costas goes to phone the car hire company.

Hire co:	Εμπρός;
	embros?
Costas:	Με λένε Κώστα Κιτάνο – νοικιάσαμε ένα αυτοκίνητο
	me lene Kosta Kitano – nikiasame ena aftokinito
	το πρωΐ – **τώρα έχει μία βλάβη.**
	to proi – tora ehi mia vlavi.
Hire co:	**Τι έγινε, κύριε;**
	ti egine, kirie?
Costas:	Ήτανε εντάξει στην αρχή, αλλά μετά η μηχανή σταμάτησε
	itane endaksi stin arhi, ala meta i mihani stamatise
	ξαφνικά και δεν ξεκινάει.
	ksafnika ke then ksekinai.
Hire co:	Που είστε ακριβώς;
	poo iste akrivos?
Costas:	Περίπου πέντε χιλιόμετρα έξω απο την πόλη.
	peripoo pende hiliometra ekso apo tin poli.
Hire co:	Εντάξει – υπάρχει ένα γκαράζ ένα χιλιόμετρο πιο κάτω στο
	endaksi – iparhi ena garaj ena hiliometro pyo kato sto
	δρόμο. Θα τους τηλεφωνήσω να στείλουν κάποιον να σας
	thromo. tha toos telefoniso na stiloon kapyon na sas
	βοηθήσει.
	voithisi.
Costas:	Ευχαριστώ. Πέστε του να έρθει γρήγορα.
	efharisto. peste too na erthi grigora.
Maria:	Ήμουνα σίγουρη ότι θα είχαμε προβλήματα!
	imoona sigoori oti tha ihame provlimata!

6 ON THE ROAD

Useful words and phrases from the dialogue

Εμπρός	embros	hello (answering phone)
με λένε	me lene	my name is
νοικιάσαμε	nikiasame	we hired
το πρωί	to proi	this morning
έχει μια βλάβη	ehi mia vlavi	we've had a breakdown
τι έγινε;	ti egine	what happened?
ήτανε εντάξει	itane endaksi	It was OK
στην αρχή	stin arhi	at the start/beginning
αλλά μετά	ala meta	but afterwards
η μηχανή	i mihani	the engine
σταμάτησε ξαφνικά	stamatise ksafnika	stopped suddenly
δεν ξεκινάει	then ksekinai	it doesn't start
ακριβώς	akrivos	exactly
έξω απο την πόλη	ekso apo tin poli	(5 km) outside the town
κάποιος -οια -οιο	kapios -ia -io	someone
να σας βοηθήσει	na sas voithisi	to help you
πέστε του	peste too	tell him
γρήγορα	grigora	quickly
ήμουνα σίγουρη	imoona sigoori	I was sure (fem.)

Problems with the car

το πλησιέστερο γκαράζ
to plisiestero garaj
the nearest garage

ο γερανός
o yeranos
breakdown truck

... δεν δουλεύει
... then thoolevi
the ... isn't working

ο αριθμός κυκλοφορίας
o arithmos kikloforias
reg. number

Μπορώ να χρησιμοποιήσω το τηλέφωνό σας;
boro na hrisimopi-iso to tilefono sas?
can I use your telephone?

Μπορείτε να με βοηθήσετε;
borite na me voithisete?
can you help me?

Τελείωσε η βενζίνη
teliose i venzini
I've run out of petrol

Έπαθα μια βλάβη στο
epatha mia vlavi sto ...
I've had a breakdown at ...

Μπορείτε να στείλετε ένα μηχανικό;
borite na stilete ena mihaniko?
can you send a mechanic?

Μπορείτε να επιδιορθώσετε ..;
borite na epithiorthosete ...
can you repair ..?

ο/η/το ... είναι σπασμένος -η -ο
o/i/to ... ine spasmenos -i -o
the ... is broken

Έσκασε το λάστιχο
eskase to lastiho
I've had a puncture

Μπορείτε να αλλάξετε το λάστιχο;
borite na alaksete to lastiho?
can you change the tyre?

For parts of the car, see topic vocabulary, page 97. General motoring
phrases, see page 76.

USING THE TELEPHONE

Telephoning in Greece   Callboxes have either a blue sign (for domestic calls) or an orange one (for international calls).

For local calls most Greeks will stop at a kiosk and use the phone that is usually provided at the side. You make your call, then pay the kiosk owner.

Cafes and restaurants often have compact red pay phones, again for local calls – put in 10 drachmas.

For international calls you can either use your hotel, which will probably be expensive, or go to the OTE (equivalent of British Telecom), where there are public cubicles. Card phones have been introduced in Greece – you buy cards with 100 units from kiosks.

Some useful phone numbers

166	ambulance/first aid – Casualty Hospital, 2 Nikis Street, Kifissia, Athens 801 4411
171	tourist police
199	fire service
104/174	ELPA (=AA/RAC) main office Athens 779 1615
144	airport information or Athens 969 9466, 981 1201
362 6970	YMCA, 28 Omirou Street, Athens
362 4291	YWCA, 11 Amerikis Street, Athens
512 4910	Long distance buses
143	Sea travel information, Pireus – also 451 1311, 451 1130, 417 2657
145/147	rail travel – also 821 3882, 513 1601
4280001-10	Flying Dolphins hydrofoil service

6 ACCIDENT AND EMERGENCY

Telephoning phrases

με συνδέετε με ...	me sintheete me ...	put me through to ...
Θέλω να μιλήσω στον/στην ...	thelo na miliso ston/stin ...	I want to speak to ...
Εμπρός – εδώ (Γιώργος)	embros – etho (Yorgos)	hello, (George) here
Πήρατε λάθος αριθμό	pirate lathos arithmo	wrong number
Πάρτε αργότερα	parte argotera	call later
Δεν απαντάει	then apandai	no answer
Το τηλέφωνο δεν λειτουργεί	to tilefono then litooryi	out of order
Σας ζητάνε στο τηλέφωνο	sas zitane sto tilefono	there's a call for you
Μιλάει	milai	(the line is) engaged (lit. he/she is speaking)

Accidents Accidents can happen, so take care, especially when hiring small motorcycles on the islands. Island roads are rarely lit at night, and the road surfaces can be uneven. Take care also when participating in water sports.

For most people the worst problems will be sunburn and stomach upsets – not from the tap water, which is fine, but from over-indulgence!

Greeks treat the midday sun (12–3 pm) with the greatest respect, so take their advice. Tan gradually, use a lotion with quite a high protection factor, and cover your head if no shade is available.

Greeks rarely drink alcohol without eating – not a bad rule to follow!

Health care in Greece As a matter of course, make sure you have good medical insurance before you leave. Few islands have full hospital emergency services. Private doctors and treatment can be expensive.

1 Police Emergency
2 Coastguard Emergency
3 Duty Doctors (Athens–Pireus)
4 Emergency Hospitals
5 First Aid Centre
6 Dental Emergency
7 Poison Centre
8 Fire Brigade

ΤΗΛΕΦΩΝΑ ΑΝΑΓΚΗΣ

1	Άμεση Δράση Αστυνομίας	100
2	Άμεση Επέμβαση Λιμενικού	108
3	Εφημ/ντες γιατροί: Αθηνών	
	Πειραιώς	105
4	Εφημερεύοντα Νοσοκομεία	106
5	Κέντρο Άμεσης Βοηθείας	166
6	Οδοντιατρείο	6434001
7	Δηλητηριάσεων	7793777
8	Πυροσβεστική	199

Useful words and phrases

(See topic vocabulary for parts of the body. Also pages 52–53 for information and vocabulary on Chemists.)

Δεν είμαι/αισθάνομαι καλά	then ime/esthanome kala	I don't feel well
είμαι άρρωστος -η	ime arostos -i	I'm ill
έπαθα δυστύχημα	epatha thistihima	I've had an accident
στραμπούληξα τον αστράγαλο	strabooliksa ton astragalo	I've sprained my ankle
έκαψα το/τη...	ekapsa to/ti...	I've burnt my...
έκοψα το/τη...	ekopsa to/ti...	I've cut my...
κόπηκα	kopika	I've cut myself
με πονάει ο/η/το...	me ponai o/i/to...	my... hurts
έχω ένα πόνο εδώ	eho ena pono etho	I have a pain here
έπεσα	epesa	I've fallen
είναι πρησμένο	ine prismeno	it's swollen
έχω πυρετό	eho pireto	I've got a temperature
έκανα εμετό	ekana emeto	I've been sick
είμαι καρδιακός/η	ime karthiakos/i	I have a heart condition
έχασα τα χάπια μου	ehasa ta hapia moo	I've lost my pills
το φάρμακο	to farmako	medicine
είμαι έγκυος	ime engios	I'm pregnant
Είμαι διαβητικός -η	ime thiavitikos -i	I'm diabetic
Με πονάει το δόντι μου	Me ponai to thondi moo	I've got toothache
παίρνω αντισυλληπτικά χάπια	perno andisiliptika hapia	I'm on the pill
Η γυναίκα μου περιμένει μωρό	i yineka moo perimeni moro	My wife is expecting a baby
Είμαι αλλεργικός/η στην πενικιλλίνη	ime aleryikos/i stin penikilini	I'm allergic to penicillin
Νομίζω ότι ο/η/το... είναι σπασμένος/η/ο	nomizo oti o/i/to... ine spasmenos/i/o	I think my... is broken
Θέλω ένα γιατρό οδοντογιατρό	thelo ena yatro othondoyatro	I want a doctor dentist
Υπάρχει γιατρός στο/στη	iparhi yatros sto/sti	Is there a doctor in...
το ιατρείο	to iatrio	surgery
το νοσοκομείο	to nosokomio	hospital
Είναι επείγον	ine epigon	it's urgent
κάνετε γρήγορα	kanete grigora	please hurry
Χρειάζομαι ένα ασθενοφόρο	hriazome ena asthenoforo	I need an ambulance
Χρειάζομαι ένα γιατρό που να μιλάει Αγγλικά	hriazome ena yatro poo na milai anglika	I need an English-speaking doctor

Other emergencies

Η αστυνομία	i astinomia	police
το αστυνομικό τμήμα	to astonomiko tmima	police station
η σύγκρουση	i singroosi	car accident/crash
Τηλεφωνείστε στην αστυνομία αμέσως	tilefoniste stin astinomia amesos	Call the police immediately
Θέλω ένα διερμηνέα	thelo ena thierminea	I want an interpreter

6 ACCIDENT AND EMERGENCY

Έχασα το πορτοφόλι μου	*ehasa to portofoli moo*	I've lost my wallet
Χάθηκε το παιδί μου	*hathike to pethi moo*	My child's got lost
Μου έκλεψαν το ... μου	*moo eklepsan to . . . moo*	Someone's stolen my ...
η πρεσβεία	*i prezvia*	embassy/consulate
η φωτιά	*i fotia*	fire
η πυροσβεστική αντλία	*i pirosvestiki andlia*	fire brigade .
ο πυροσβέστης	*o pirosvestis*	fireman
Το δωμάτιό μου έπιασε φωτιά	*to thomatio moo epyase fotia*	my room is on fire

ο ναυαγοσώστης	*o navagosostis*	lifeguard
Το παιδί μου δεν ξέρει κολύμπι	*to pethi moo then kseri kolimbi*	my child can't swim
Βοήθεια	*voithia*	help!
πνίγεται	*pniyete*	he/she's drowning!

the way it works

Past tense

The past tense of the verb **είμαι**/*ime*, to be, is as follows:

ήμουν(α)	*imoon(a)*	I was
ήσουν(α)	*isoon(a)*	you were
ήταν(ε)	*itan(e)*	he/she/it was
ήμαστε	*imaste*	we were
ήσαστε	*isaste*	you were
ήταν(ε)	*itan(e)*	they were

The final (*e*) can be included or omitted.

The past tense of the verb **έχω**/*eho*, I have, is as follows:

είχα	*iha*	I had
είχες	*ihes*	you had
είχε	*ihe*	he/she/it had
είχαμε	*ihame*	we had
είχατε	*ihate*	you had
είχαν(ε)	*ihan(e)*	they had

The endings shown above for the past of **έχω**/*eho*, are typical of past tense endings for most other verbs, e.g.:

Ήμαστε στην Ελλάδα πέρυσι
imaste stin elatha perisi
We were in Greece last year

6 ACCIDENT AND EMERGENCY

Ο Γιώργος δεν ήτανε στην ταβέρνα χθές
o Yorgos then itane stin taverna hthes
George was not in the taverna yesterday

Είχαμε ένα πρόβλημα με το αυτοκίνητο την περασμένη εβδομάδα
ihame ena provlima me to aftokinito tin perasmeni evthomatha
We had a problem with the car last week

Είχα πολλή δουλειά πριν τις διακοπές μου
iha poli thoolia prin tis thiakopes moo
I had a lot of work before my holidays

To form the past tense, add the following endings to the future stem.
Remember that most verbs change their form in the future, e.g.
Θα αγοράσω/*tha agoraso*. It is the future stem which is used to form the past
tense.

αγόρασα	*agóras -a*	I bought
αγόρασες	*-es*	you bought
αγόρασε	*-e*	he/she bought
αγοράσαμε	*-ame*	we bought
αγοράσατε	*-ate*	you bought
αγόρασαν	*-an*	they bought

Note that the stress is shifted to the syllable before that stressed in the
present tense: **αγοράζω**/*agorAzo* (present), **αγόρασα**/*agOrasa* (past).

In the past tense the third syllable before the end of the word is always
stressed. There are some verbs that consist only of two syllables in the
present, e.g. **παίζω**/*pezo*, I play. In these cases, the prefix -**ε**/-*e* is added to
the front of the verb and it is stressed, e.g. **παίζω**/*pEzo* (present) becomes
έπαιξα/*Epeksa*, I played.

Examples of the past tense from this unit:

Present		*Past*	
νοικιάζω	*nikiAzo*	**νοίκιασα**	*nIkiasa*
σταματάω	*stamatAO*	**σταμάτησα**	*stamAtisa*
πληρώνω	*plirOno*	**πλήρωσα**	*plIrosa*
ξεκινάω	*ksekinAO*	**ξεκίνησα**	*ksekInisa*
τηλεφωνώ	*tilefonO*	**τηλεφώνησα**	*tilefOnissa*
στέλνω	*stElno*	**έστειλα**	*Estila*

Some examples

Πληρώσαμε 5.000 δρχ. στο εστιατόριο!   We paid 5.000 dr. in the restaurant!
Plirosame 5.000 dr. sto estiatorio!

Έστειλες κάρτες στο γραφείο σου;   Did you send cards to your office?
Estiles kartes sto grafio soo?

Δεν τηλεφώνησαν στο σπίτι τους χθές   They didn't phone home yesterday
Then tilefonisan sto spiti toos hthes

6 ACCIDENT AND EMERGENCY

things to do

6.3 Using the verbs given in the past tense, translate the words in brackets into Greek and match them with the column on the right:

1 Η βενζίνη (has run out)
2 (I've had) μια βλάβη
3 Το αυτοκίνητο (stopped) ξαφνικά
4 (He's lost) το πορτοφόλι του
5 (They stole) το διαβατήριό μου
6 (I've cut) το δάχτυλό μου

a σταμάτησε
b έκλεψαν
c έκοψα
d έπαθα
e έχασε
f τελείωσε

6.4 Match the sentences with the parts of the body shown:

1 Έκοψα το δάχτυλό μου
2 Με πονάει το δόντι μου
3 Έπαθα έγκαυμα
4 Το πόδι μου είναι πρησμένο
5 Έχω πονοκέφαλο
6 Με πονάει το στομάχι μου

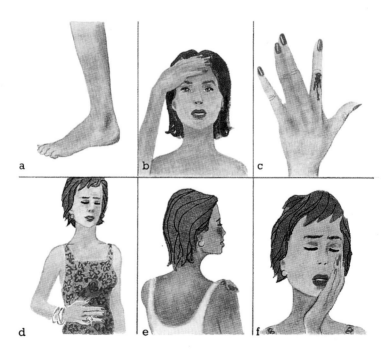

7 SOCIAL MATTERS

GREEK FESTIVALS

Being an Orthodox country, the Greek calendar is punctuated by many saint's days. As most people are named after saints – Giorgos (George), Maria, etc. – they will celebrate their 'name day' on the saint's day. This is in addition to their natural birthday. Cards and presents are exchanged on name days.

The central event in Greek traditional life is Easter. This is preceded by celebrations and festivities during Carnival, where people dress up and go out in boisterous groups (especially in the Plaka area); this festival is followed by Lent.

Easter begins with processions on Good Friday, and culminates in the midnight announcement 'Christ is risen!' (**Χριστός Ανέστη!**/*Hristos anesti!*) when people make a candlelight procession home from church. Traditionally lambs are roasted on a spit, and feasting ensues.

Cultural events   Athens holds the Athens Festival of Music and Drama every summer, July to September. It is centred around the Herod Atticus Theatre (at the foot of the Acropolis), and offers a variety of classical and modern concerts, ballets and drama. Performances start at 21.00.

Epidavros – the ancient centre of Greek drama, situated 150 km south of Athens in the Peloponnese – has a drama festival every summer. Excusions are plentiful from Athens, combining theatre tickets with visits to ancient sites. Not to be missed.

7 SOCIAL MATTERS

For those with a thirst, don't miss a visit to the Wine Festival, which runs throughout the summer at Daphni, a few miles outside Athens. There's free wine to taste, and folk dancing to enjoy. Your hotel, and the Greek Tourist Office will have details. Coach trips are organised there regularly.

Public holidays in Greece

January 1	New Year
January 6	Epiphany
1st Monday of March	'Clean Monday' – 1st day of Lent
March 25	National Holiday – Independence Day
Easter Sunday, Monday	
May 1	Labour Day
August 15	Assumption
October 28	Όχι 'No' Day – national holiday, when the Greeks resisted the invasion of the Italians in 1941.

Days of the week

η Κυριακή	i kiriaki	Sunday	η Πέμπτη	i pempti	Thursday
η Δευτέρα	i deftera	Monday	η Παρασκευή	i paraskevi	Friday
η Τρίτη	i triti	Tuesday	το Σάββατο	to savato	Saturday
η Τετάρτη	i tetarti	Wednesday			

Seasons

η άνοιξη	i aniksi	Spring	το φθινόπωρο	to fthinoporo	Autumn
το καλοκαίρι	to kalokeri	Summer	ο χειμώνας	o himonas	Winter

Months of the year

There are two forms – both are masculine

Ιανουάριος	ianooarios	Γενάρης	yenaris	January
Φεβρουάριος	fevrooarios	Φλεβάρης	flevaris	February
Μάρτιος	martios	Μάρτης	martis	March
Απρίλιος	aprilios	Απρίλης	aprilis	April
Μάϊος	maios	Μάης	mais	May
Ιούνιος	ioonios	Ιούνης	ioonis	June
Ιούλιος	ioolios	Ιούλης	ioolis	July
Αύγουστος	avgoostos			August
Σεπτέμβριος	septemvrios	Σεπτέμβρης	septemvris	September
Οκτώβριος	oktovrios	Οκτώβρης	oktovris	October
Νοέμβριος	noemvrios	Νοέμβρης	noemvris	November
Δεκέμβριος	thekemvrios	Δεκέμβρης	thekemvris	December

Πόσο του μηνός έχουμε σήμερα;	posso too minos ehoome simera?	What's the date today?
Είκοσι μία Μαρτίου	ikosi mia martioo	21st March

7 SOCIAL MATTERS

SAYING GOODBYE

Μέχρι την επόμενη φορά/Until the next time

Peter is leaving soon, and has to tear himself away from Maria!

Maria: Τι κρίμα που φεύγεις σήμερα!
ti krima poo fevyis simera!

Peter: Και εγώ λυπάμαι. Πήγαμε σε τόσα ωραία μέρη. Φάγαμε όλα
ke ego lipame. Pigame se tossa orea meri. Fagame ola
τα ελληνικά φαγητά, και ήπιαμε τα καλύτερα κρασιά.
ta elinika fagita, ke ipyame ta kalitera krasya.

Costas: Χαίρομαι που σου άρεσε τόσο πολύ η Ελλάδα.
herome poo soo arese tosso poli i elatha.

Peter: Και οι Ελληνίδες (looking at Maria) μ'άρεσαν πολύ.
ke i elinithes m'aresan poli.

Maria: Μπορεί να σε δούμε στην Αγγλία φέτος.
bori na se thoume stin anglia fetos.

Peter: **Πότε θα έρθετε; Θα ήθελα να σας δείξω το Λονδίνο.** Έχετε
pote tha erthete. tha ithela na sas thikso to lonthino. ehete
τη διεύθυνσή μου. Τηλεφωνείστε μου.
ti thiefthinsi moo – telefoniste moo.

Costas: (interrupting) Λοιπόν, Peter. **Χάρηκα που σε γνώρισα.** Καλό
lipon, Peter. harika poo se gnorisa. kalo
ταξίδι, και καλό χειμώνα.
taksithi, ke kalo himona.

Maria: Θα μου λείψεις Peter. Έλα ξανά γρήγορα.
tha moo lipsis, Peter. ela ksana grigora.

Peter: Αντίο σας, **μέχρι την επόμενη φορά.**
adio sas, mehri tin epomeni fora.

7 SOCIAL MATTERS

Useful words and phrases from the dialogue

Τι κρίμα!	*ti krima*	what a pity!
Λυπάμαι	*lipame*	I regret (it)/I'm sorry
Πήγαμε	*pigame*	we went
σε τόσα ωραία μέρη	*se tossa orea meri*	to so many nice places
Φάγαμε	*fagame*	we ate
Ήπιαμε	*ipyame*	we drank
τα καλύτερα κρασιά	*ta kalitera krasia*	the best wines
Χαίρομαι	*herome*	I'm glad
Σου άρεσε	*soo arese*	you liked
Η Ελληνίδα -ες	*i elinitha -es*	Greek woman/women
Μπορεί	*bori*	maybe
Φέτος	*fetos*	this year
Πότε θα έρθετε;	*pote tha erthete?*	when will you come?
Να σας δείξω	*na sas thikso*	to show you
Χάρηκα που σε γνώρισα	*harika poo se gnorisa*	glad to have met you
Καλό ταξίδι	*kalo taksithi*	bon voyage
Καλό χειμώνα	*kalo himona*	have a good winter
Θα μου λείψεις	*tha moo lipsis*	I'll miss you
Έλα ξανά γρήγορα	*ela ksana grigora*	come back quickly
αντίο	*adio*	goodbye
Μέχρι την επόμενη φορά	*mehri tin epomeni fora*	until the next time

Other useful phrases

Ελπίζω να σε/σας ξαναδώ σύντομα
elpizo na se/sas ksanatho sindoma
I hope to see you again soon

Λυπάμαι που δεν μπορείς/μπορείτε να μείνεις/μείνετε
lipame poo then boris/borite na minis/minete
I'm sorry you can't stay

Θα έρθεις του χρόνου, μου το υπόσχεσαι;
tha erthis too hronoo, moo to ipos-hese?
You'll come next year, do you promise me?

Πρέπει να φύγω/φύγουμε
prepi na figo/figoome
I/we have to leave

7 SOCIAL MATTERS

Ασφαλώς θα έρθω ξανά
Of course I'll come again

Anne is at a bouzouki place with Yiannis and Eleni Vazakas and friends. It's her last evening in Athens.

Friend:	**Να σας συστηθώ. Σπύρος Νουσίου.** *na sas sistitho. Spiros Noosioo.*
Anne:	Ann Johnson. Χαίρω πολύ. **Είμαι η φίλη του κύριου Βαζάκα.** *Anne Johnson. hero poli. ime i fili too kirioo vazaka.*
Friend:	Πρώτη φορά έρχεστε στην Ελλάδα; *proti fora erheste stin elatha?*
Anne:	Ναι. Πέρασα μια θαυμάσια εβδομάδα στην Αθήνα. *ne. perasa mia thavmasia evthomatha stin athina.*
Friend:	Πως σας φάνηκε ο ελληνικός καιρός; *pos sas fanike o elinikos keros?*
Anne:	Ήτανε θαυμάσιος! Βέβαια, έκανε πολύ ζέστη αλλά αυτό *Itane thavmasios! Vevea, ekane poli zesti ala afto* θέλουμε εμείς οι Άγγλοι. *theloome emis i angli.*
Eleni:	Πως πέρασες στις διακοπές σου Ann; *pos perases stis thiakopes soo Anne?*
Anne:	**Χάρη σε σας, είδα όλα τα αξιοθέατα της Αθήνας. Πάντα θα** *hari se sas, itha ola ta aksiotheata tis athinas. panda tha* θυμάμαι το ταξίδι που κάναμε στους Δελφούς. *thimame to taksithi poo kaname stoos thelfoos.*
Yiannis:	**Ας πιούμε στην υγεία της Anne. Να έρθεις ξανά του χρόνου.** *as pyoome stin iyia tis Anne. na erthis Ksana too hronoo.*
Anne:	**Ασφαλώς θα έρθω ξανά. Ευχαριστώ για όλα.** *asfalos tha ertho ksana. efharisto ya ola.*

7 SOCIAL MATTERS

Useful words and phrases from the dialogue

Να σας συστηθώ	na sas sistitho	let me introduce myself
ο φίλος/η φίλη	o filos, i fili	friend (masc./fem.)
πέρασα	perasa	I've spent
Πως σας φάνηκε;	pos sas fanike	How did ... seem to you?
Χάρη σε σας	hari se sas	thanks to you
Είδα	itha	I saw
τα αξιοθέατα	ta aksiotheata	the sights
Πάντα θα θυμάμαι	panda tha thimame	I'll always remember
που κάναμε	poo kaname	that we made
Να έρθεις ξανά	na erthis ksana	Come again
Ας πιούμε στην υγειά	as pyoome stin iyia	let's drink to health
του χρόνου	too hronoo	next year
Ασφαλώς θα έρθω ξανά	Asfalos tha ertho ksana	Of course I'll come again

Socializing

Έχετε παιδιά;	ehete pethia?	Do you have any children?
Έχω ένα γιό και μια κόρη	eho ena yo ke mia kori	I have a son and a daughter
Πόσων χρονών είναι;	poson hronon ine?	How old is/are he/she/they?
Είστε παντρεμένος/η;	iste pandremenos/i?	Are you married?

Farewells

ο κύριος και κυρία ... ήτανε πολύ καλοί μαζί μου	Mr and Mrs ... have been very good to me
o kirios ke i kiria ... itane poli kali mazi moo	
Όταν έρθετε στην Αγγλία θα μείνετε στο σπίτι μου	When you come to England you'll stay at my house
otan erthete stin anglia tha minete sto spiti moo	
Μακάρι να έμενα ακόμη μια εβδομάδα	I wish I could stay another week
makari na emena akomi mia evthomatha	

things to do

7.1 **a** You are telling a Greek friend what you liked and didn't like during your holiday:

1 Greek food/liked
2 traffic in Athens/didn't like
3 Greek people/liked
4 stuffed vine leaves/didn't like

b and what you and your friends did:

5 We went to Sounion.
6 We saw the Acropolis.

7 SOCIAL MATTERS

7 We ate moussaka every day (!)
8 We drank retsina every night (!!)
9 We went on (lit. made) a trip to Epidavros.
10 We had a wonderful time!

7.2 You are at a party with some Greek people:

Greek: **Να σας συστηθώ. Με λένε Δημήτρη Τσεκούρα.**
You: (introduce yourself)
Greek: **Μιλάτε ελληνικά πολύ καλά. Απο που είστε;**
You: (say where you're from)
Greek: **Σας αρέσει η Ελλάδα;**
You: (of course you do – say it's your second time)
Greek: **Σε ποιά νησιά πήγατε;**
You: (say you went to Aegina, Hydra and Poros)
Greek: **Θα έρθετε ξανά του χρόνου;**
You: 'say you'll come back, certainly)

KEY TO EXERCISES

1.1 1 Καλημέρα σας.
2 Καλησπέρα σας. 3 Γειά σου.
4 Γειά σας/χαίρετε.
1.2 1 Θέλω ένα μονόκλινο.
2 Θέλω ένα δίκλινο. 3 Θέλω ένα δίκλινο με ντους. 4 Θέλω ένα μονόκλινο με μπάνιο. 5 Θέλω ένα τρίκλινο με μπάνιο.
1.3 You: Καλημέρα. You: Το όνομά μου είναι … You: Ορίστε το διαβατήριό μου. You: Τι ώρα έχει πρωϊνό;
1.4 1 τρία. 2 δώδεκα
3 δεκαεπτά. 4 δέκα.
5 δεκατέσσερα.
1.5 1 Θέλω τσάϊ με γάλα, αυγά και μπέϊκον. 2 Θέλει καφέ, τόστ και μαρμελάδα, 3 Θέλουμε πορτοκαλάδα. 4 Θέλει τσάϊ με λεμόνι, τόστ, βραστό αυγό.

2.1 You: Απο την Αγγλία.
You: Είμαι … You: Ναι, με τη γυναίκα μου/άντρα μου/με μερικούς φίλους. You: Τρεις μέρες.
You: Στο ξενοδοχείο "Ακρόπολη".
2.2 1 Τι ώρα φτάνει …
Answer Φτάνει στις δέκα και μισή.
2 … φεύγει … **Answer** Φεύγει στις έντεκα παρά τέταρτο. 3 Πόση ώρα κάνει … **Answer** Κάνει μια ώρα και δεκαπέντε λεπτά. 4 Πόσα λεωφορεία πηγαίνουν;
Answer Πέντε.
2.3 1 Η ώρα είναι τρεις το πρωί.
2 Η ώρα είναι οκτώ και μισή το πρωί. 3 Η ώρα είναι δώδεκα παρά πέντε το μεσημέρι. 4 Η ώρα είναι δώδεκα το μεσημέρι. 5 Η ώρα είναι δύο και μισή το απόγευμα. 6 Η ώρα είναι έξι και μισή το βράδυ.

3.1 1 ένα μέτριο. 2 ένα σκέτο, ένα γλυκό. 3 δύο μέτριους. 4 μια μπύρα. 5 δύο μπύρες. 6 τρεις κόκα-κόλες.
3.2 You: Το λογαριασμό, παρακαλώ. You: Συγγνώμη, δύο μπύρες, ένα τόστ. You: Πόσο κάνουν; You: Ορίστε τέσσερις χιλιάδες δραχμές … Εντάξει.

3.3 You: μια καλαμαράκια, μια χταπόδι, μια ταραμοσαλάτα.
You: μισό κιλό μπαρμπούνια και δύο πατάτες τηγανητές. You: ένα μπουκάλι ρετσίνα και μια σόδα.
You: και μιά χωριάτικη, παρακαλώ
Total bill 11.650 δρχ.
3.4 1b. 2e. 3f. 4a. 5d. 6c.

4.1 1c. 2d. 3a. 4b.
4.2 1 ένα κιλό μήλα. 2 δύο κονσέρβες χυμό ντομάτα. 3 ένα πακέτο ζάχαρη. 4 ένα λίτρο νερό.
4.3 1 Δεν μ'αρέσει το χταπόδι.
2 Μ'αρέσουν πολύ τα σταφύλια.
3 Μ'αρέσει το ελληνικό τυρί.
4 Δεν μ'αρέσουν τα Ελληνικά τσιγάρα.
4.4 You Έχετε αυτά τα παπούτσια στο μέγεθός μου; You: Στην Αγγλία είμαι μέγεθος έξι. Τι μέγεθος είναι αυτό στην Ελλάδα;
You: Μ'αρέσουν τα μπλέ.
You: Είναι λίγο μεγάλα. Μπορώ να δοκιμάσω το μέγεθος τριάντα οχτώ; You: εντάξει, θα πάρω τα καφέ, μέγεθος τριάντα οχτώ.
4.5 1 Μπορώ να δω τον κατάλογο, παρακαλώ; 2 Μπορούμε να έχουμε ένα τραπέζι για τέσσερις, παρακαλώ; 3 Που μπορώ να βρώ ένα φαρμακείο; 4 Μπορώ να δοκιμάσω αυτό το φόρεμα παρακαλώ;

5.1 1 Τι ώρα φεύγει το πλοίο;
2 Πόσο κάνει το εισιτήριο;
3 Πόση ώρα κάνει το ταξίδι; 4 Τι ώρα γυρίζει το πλοίο; 5 Που θα φάμε μεσημεριανό; 6 Πρέπει να αγοράσω τα εισιτήρια τώρα;
5.2 You: Είναι ελεύθερη αυτή η θέση; You: Οχι, πρέπει να κατεβώ στη Γλυφάδα. You: Οχι, δεν είμαι σίγουρος/η. Μπορείτε να μου πείτε που να κατεβώ; You: Ναι, αλλά φεύγω σε δύο μέρες.

KEY TO EXERCISES

5.3 1 Υπάρχουν θέσεις για απόψε;
2 Πόσο κάνουν τα εισιτήρια;
3 Θέλω τέσσερα εισιτήρια.
4 Πόσο κάνουν όλα μαζί; 5 Τι
ώρα αρχίζει η παράσταση; Τι ώρα
τελειώνει η παράσταση;
5.4 You: Τι παίζει στο σινεμά
απόψε; **You:** Τι άλλο μπορούμε να
κάνουμε; **You:** Πρέπει να κλείσουμε
τραπέζι; **You:** Ναι, ένα τραπέζι για
δύο στις εννιά και μισή.

6.1 You: Θέλω να νοικιάσω … με
τέσσερις πόρτες. **You:** … ένα φτηνό
αυτοκίνητο. **You:** Πόσο κάνει για
μιά ημέρα; **You:** Για τρεις μέρες.
6.2 1 Γεμίστε το με σούπερ.
2 Ελέγξτε το λάδι παρακαλώ.
3 Πάει αυτός ο δρόμος στην
Αθήνα; 4 Πόσα χιλιόμετρα είναι
μέχρι την Αθήνα;

6.3 1f. 2d. 3a. 4e. 5b. 6c.
6.4 1c. 2f. 3e. 4a. 5b. 6d.

7.1 1 Μ'άρεσε το ελληνικό
φαγητό. 2 Δεν μ'άρεσε η κίνηση
στην Αθήνα. 3 Μ'άρεσαν οι
Έλληνες. 4 Δεν μ'άρεσαν οι
ντολμάδες. 5 Πήγαμε στο Σούνιο.
6 Είδαμε την Ακρόπολη.
7 Φάγαμε μουσακά κάθε μέρα.
8 Ήπιαμε ρετσίνα κάθε βράδυ.
9 Κάναμε ένα ταξίδι στην
Επίδαυρο. 10 Περάσαμε πολύ
ωραία.
7.2 You: Με λένε … **You:** Είμαι
απο … **You:** Ασφαλώς – Είναι η
δεύτερη φορά που έρχομαι.
You: Πήγα στην Αίγινα, στην
Ύδρα και στον Πόρο.
You: Ασφαλώς θα έρθω ξανά.

TOPIC VOCABULARY

ENGLISH–GREEK WORDLISTS

Professions/jobs

accountant	*logistis*/**λογιστ-ής** (m.), **-ρια** (f.)
archeologist	*arheologos*/**αρχαιολόγος** (m./f.)
bank clerk	*ipalilos trapezis*/**υπάλληλος Τραπέζης** (m./f.)
businessman/woman	*epihirimatias*/**επιχειρηματίας** (m./f.)
civil servant	*thimosios ipalilos*/**δημόσιος υπάλληλος** (m./f.)
computer operator	*hiristis kompiooter*/**χειριστ-ής** (m.), **-ρια** (f.) **κομπιούτερ**
dentist	*othondiatros*/**οδοντίατρος** (m./f.)
designer	*shethiastis*/**σχεδιαστ-ής** (m.), **-ρια** (f.)
director	*thiefthindis*/**διευθυντ-ής** (m.), **-ρια** (f.)
doctor	*giatros*/**γιατρός** (m./f.)
electrician	*ilectrologos*/**ηλεκτρολόγος** (m.)
employee	*ipalilos*/**υπάλληλος** (m./f.)
engineer	*mihanikos*/**μηχανικός** (m./f.)
factory worker	*ergat-is/-ria ergostasiou*/**εργάτ-ης** (m), **-ρια** (f.) **εργοστασίου**
farmer	*agrotis*/**αγρότ-ης** (m.) **-ρια** (f.)
hairdresser	*komotis*/**κομμωτ-ής** (m.), **-ρια** (f.)
housewife	*nikokira*/**νοικοκυρά** (f.)
interpreter	*thiermineas*/**διερμηνέας** (m./f.)
journalist	*thimosiografos*/**δημοσιογράφος** (m./f.)
lawyer	*thikigoros*/**δικηγόρος** (m./f.)
mechanic	*tehnitis*/**τεχνίτης** (m.)
nurse	*ηosokoma*/**νοσοκόμα** (f.)
plumber	*ithravlikos*/**υδραυλικός** (m.)
policeman	*astinomikos*/**αστυνομικός** (m.)
retired	*sintaksioohos*/**συνταξιούχος** (m./f.)
sales rep	*andiprosopos poliseon*/**αντιπρόσωπος πωλήσεων**
secretary	*gramateas*/**γραμματέας** (m./f.)
shop assistant	*ipalilos katastimatos*/**υπάλληλος καταστήματος**
social worker	*kinonik-os/-i litoorgos*/**κοινωνικ-ός** (m.), **-ή** (f.) **λειτουργός**
teacher	*thaskalos*/**δάσκαλ-ος** (m), **-α** (f.)
technician	*tehnikos*/**τεχνικός** (m.)
unemployed	*anergos/-i*/**άνεργος** (m), **-η** (f.)

Clothes

bag	*tsanda*/**τσάντα** (f.)
belt	*zoni*/**ζώνη** (f.)
bikini	*bikini*/**μπικίνι** (n.)
blouse	*blooza*/**μπλούζα** (f.)
boots	*botes*/**μπότες** (f.)
bra	*soutien*/**σουτιέν** (n.)
briefs/pants	*kilota*/**κυλότα** (f.)
cardigan	*jaketa*/**ζακέττα** (f.)
coat	*palto*/**παλτό** (n.)
dress	*forema*/**φόρεμα** (n.)
gloves	*gandia*/**γάντια** (n.)
handkerchief	*mandili*/**μαντήλι** (n.)
hat	*kapelo*/**καπέλλο** (n.)

TOPIC VOCABULARY

jacket	*zaketa*/**ζακέτα** (f.)
jeans	*gins*/**τζήνς**
jumper	*blooza*/**μπλούζα** (f.)
nightdress	*nihtiko*/**νυχτικό** (n.)
pyjamas	*pitzames*/**πυτζάμες** (f.)
raincoat	*athiavroho*/**αδιάβροχο** (n.)
sandals	*pethila*/**πέδιλα** (n.)
scarf	*kaskol*/**κασκώλ** (n.)
shirt	*pookamiso*/**πουκάμισο** (n.)
shoes	*papootsia*/**παπούτσια** (n.)
skirt	*foosta*/**φούστα** (f.)
slippers	*pandofles*/**παντόφλες** (f.)
stockings	*kaltses*/**κάλτσες** (f.)
suit men	*kostoomi*/**κοστούμι** (n.)
women	*tayier*/**ταγιέρ** (n.)
sweatshirt	*fanela*/**φανέλλα** (f.)
swimming costume	*magio*/**μαγιώ** (n.)
teeshirt	*mako blooza*/**μακώ μπλούζα** (f.)
tie	*gravata*/**γραβάτα** (f.)
tights	*kalson*/**καλσόν** (n.)
trainers	*athlitika papootsia*/**αθλητικά παπούτσια**
trousers	*pandeloni*/**παντελόνι** (n.)

Colours

colour	*hroma*/**χρώμα** (n.)
beige	*bez*/**μπέζ** (n.)
black	*mavro*/**μαύρο** (n.)
blue	*ble*/**μπλέ** (n.)
brown	*kafe*/**καφέ** (n.)
green	*prasino*/**πράσινο** (n.)
grey	*gri*/**γκρί** (n.)
orange	*portokali*/**πορτοκαλί** (n.)
pink	*roz*/**ροζ** (n.)
red	*kokino*/**κόκκινο** (n.)
white	*aspro*/**άσπρο** (n.)
yellow	*kitrino*/**κίτρινο** (n.)
dark/light	*skooro/anihto*/**σκούρο/ανοιχτό**
purple	*mov, porfiro*/**μώβ** (n), **πορφυρό** (n.)

Materials

acrylic	*akrilikos*/**ακρυλικός/η/ο**
cotton	*vamvakeros*/**βαμβακερός/η/ο**
denim	*jin*/**τζην**
fur	*gooninos/i/o*/**γούνινος/η/ο**
leather	*thermatinos/i/o*/**δερμάτινος/η/ο**
nylon	*nailon*/**νάϋλον**
silk	*metaksotos/i/o*/**μεταξωτός/η/ο**
suede	*kastorinos*/**καστόρινος/η/ο**
wool	*malinos*/**μάλλινος/η/ο**

TOPIC VOCABULARY

Chemists

antimosquito burner tablet	*Spiramat*/**ΣΠΙΡΑΜΑΤ** *Spiramat tabletes*/**ΣΠΙΡΑΜΑΤ ταμπλέττες**
antiseptic	*antisiptikos/i/o*/**αντισηπτικός/η/ο**
aspirin	*aspirini*/**ασπιρίνη (f.)**
bandage	*epithesmos*/**επίδεσμος (m.)**
capsule	*kapsoola*/**κάψουλα (f.)**
condom	*profilaktiko*/**προφυλακτικό (n.)**
contraceptive	*andisiliptiko*/**αντισυλληπτικό (n.)**
contraceptive pill	*andisiliptiko hapi*/**αντισυλληπτικό χάπι (n.)**
cotton wool	*vamvaki*/**βαμβάκι (n.)**
cough syrup	*siropi yia viha*/**σιρόπι για βήχα (n.)**
eyedrops	*stagones yia ta matia*/**σταγόνες για τα μάτια**
laxative	*kathartiko*/**καθαρτικό (n.)**
medicine	*farfako*/**φάρμακο (n.)**
pain killer	*pafsipono*/**παυσίπονο (n.)**
pill	*hapi*/**χάπι (n.)**
plaster	*tsiroto, emblastro*/**τσιρότο, έμπλαστρο (n.)**
prescription	*sindayi*/**συνταγή (f.)**
sanitary towel	*servietes iyias*/**σερβιέττες υγείας (f.)**
tampon	*tampon*/**ταμπόν (n.)**
suntan lotion/oil	*andiliaki krema/lathi*/**αντηλιακή κρέμα/αντηλιακό λάδι**
suppository	*ipotheto*/**υπόθετο (n.)**
thermometer	*thermometro*/**θερμόμετρο (n.)**
throat pastilles	*pastilies yia to lemo*/**παστίλλιες για το λαιμό**

Toiletries

aftershave	*losion yia meta to ksirisma*/**λοσιόν για μετά το ξύρισμα**
baby food	*pethikes trofes*/**παιδικές τροφές**
brush	*voortsa*/**βούρτσα (f.)**
comb	*htena*/**χτένα (f.)**
contact lens	*fakos epafis*/**φακός επαφής (m.)**
cream	*krema*/**κρέμα (f.)**
deodorant	*aposmitiko*/**αποσμητικό (n.)**
disposable nappies	*panes mias hriseos*/**πάνες μιας χρήσεως**
lipstick	*krayion*/**κραγιόν (n.)**
perfume	*aroma*/**άρωμα (n.)**
razor	*ksiristiki mihani*/**ξυριστική μηχανή (f.)**
razor blade	*ksirafi*/**ξυράφι (n.)**
safety pin	*paramana*/**παραμάνα (f.)**
shampoo	*sampooan*/**σαμπουάν (n.)**
shaving cream	*krema ksirismatos*/**κρέμα ξυρίσματος (f.)**
shaving foam	*afros ksirismatos*/**αφρός ξυρίσματος (m.)**
sun glasses	*yialia ilioo*/**γυαλιά ηλίου (n.)**
tissue	*hartomandila*/**χαρτομάντηλα (n.)**
toilet paper	*harti tooalettas*/**χαρτί τουαλέττας (n.)**
toothbrush	*othondovoortsa*/**οδοντόβουρτσα (f.)**
toothpaste	*othondopasta*/**οδοντόπαστα (f.)**

TOPIC VOCABULARY

Shops

Food and drink

baker	*foornos*/**Φούρνος** (m.)
butcher	*kreopolio*/**Κρεοπωλείο** (n.)
confectioner	*zaharoplastio*/**Ζαχαροπλαστείο** (n.)
dairy	*galaktopolio*/**Γαλακτοπωλείο** (n.)
fishmonger	*psarathiko*/**Ψαράδικο** (n.)
fruiterer	*manaviko*/**Μανάβικο** (n.)
greengrocer	*manaviko*/**Μανάβικο** (n.)
grocer	*bakaliko*/**Μπακάλικο** (n.)
market	*agora*/**Αγορά** (f.)
supermarket	*soopermarket*/**Σουπερμάρκετ** (n.)
wine merchant	*kava*/**Κάβα** (f.)

other

bank	*trapeza*/**Τράπεζα** (f.)
bookshop	*vivliopolio*/**Βιβλιοπωλείο** (n.)
camping supplies	*ithi kataskinosis*/**Είδη κατασκήνωσης**
chemist	*farmakio*/**Φαρμακείο** (n.)
clothes women	*yinekia*/**Γυναικεία**
men	*andrika*/**Ανδρικά**
department store	*katastima*/**κατάστημα** (n.)
dry cleaners	*katharistirio*/**καθαριστήριο** (n.)
hairdressers	*komotirio*/**κομμωτήριο** (n.)
laundry	*plindirio*/**Πλυντήριο** (n.)
kiosk	*periptero*/**Περίπτερο** (n.)
post office	*tahithromio*/**Ταχυδρομείο** (n.)
shoe shop	*katastima papootsion*/**Κατάστημα Παπουτσιών** (n.)
stationers	*hartopolio*/**Χαρτοπωλείο** (n.)
tobacconist	*kapnopolio*/**Καπνοπωλείο** (n.)
toyshop	*katastima pehnithion*/**Κατάστημα παιχνιδιών** (n.)

Parts of a car

accelerator	*gazi*/**γκάζι** (n.)
battery	*bataria*/**μπαταρία** (f.)
bonnet/hood	*kapo*/**καπό** (n.)
boot/trunk	*port bagaz*/**πορτ μπαγκάζ** (n.)
brakes	*frena*/**φρένα** (n.)
bulb	*glombos*/**γλόμπος** (m.)
bumber/fender	*profilaktiras*/**προφυλακτήρας** (m.)
carburretor	*karbirater*/**καρμπυρατέρ** (n.)
clutch	*ambrayiaz*/**αμπραγιάζ** (n.)
dynamo	*yenitria*/**γεννήτρια** (f.)
engine	*mihani*/**μηχανή** (f.)
exhaust	*eksatmisi*/**εξάτμιση** (f.)
fan-belt	*imas*/**ιμάς** (m.)
fuse	*asfalia*/**ασφάλεια** (f.)
gear	*tahitita*/**ταχύτητα** (f.)
gearbox	*kivotio tahititon*/**κιβώτιο ταχυτήτων** (n.)

TOPIC VOCABULARY

headlight	*brostino fanari*/**μπροστινό φανάρι (n.)**
horn	*klakson*/**κλάξον (n)**
jack	*grilos*/**γρύλλος (m.)**
lights head	*brostina fota*/**μπροστινά φώτα (n.)**
rear	*piso fota*/**πίσω φώτα (n.)**
side	*plaina fota*/**πλαϊνά ψώτχ (n.)**
brake	*fota frenon*/**φώτα φρένων (n.)**
indicator	*flas*/**φλάς (n.)**
number plate	*pinakitha*/**πινακίδα (f.)**
petrol	*venzini*/**βενζίνη (f.)**
petrol tank	*deposito venzinis*/**ντεπόζιτο βενζίνης (n.)**
seat	*thesi*/**θέση (f.)**
seatbelt	*zoni asfalias*/**ζώνη ασφαλείας (f.)**
spark plug	*boozi*/**μπουζί (n.)**
starter	*ekinitir*/**εκκινητήρ (m.)**
steering wheel	*timoni*/**τιμόνι (n.)**
tyre	*lastiho*/**λάστιχο (n.)**
wheel	*rotha*/**ρόδα (f.)**
windscreen	*parbriz*/**παρμπρίζ (n.)**
windscreen wiper	*ialokatharistires*/**υαλοκαθαριστήρες (m.)**

Food

Fruit

apple	*milo*/**μήλο (n.)**
banana	*banana*/**μπανάνα (f.)**
cherry	*kerasi*/**κεράσι (n.)**
fig	*siko*/**σύκο (n.)**
grape white	*stafili aspro*/**σταφύλι άσπρο (n.)**
black	*stafili mavro*/ **μαύρο**
lemon	*lemoni*/**λεμόνι (n.)**
mandarin	*mandarini*/**μανταρίνι (n.)**
melon	*peponi*/**πεπόνι (n.)**
nectarine	*nektarini*/**νεκταρίνη (n.)**
orange	*portokali*/**πορτοκάλι (n.)**
peach	*rothakino*/**ροδάκινο (n.)**
pear	*ahlathi*/**αχλάδι (n.)**
pineapple	*ananas*/**ανανάς (m.)**
watermelon	*karpoozi*/**καρπούζι (n.)**

Vegetables

aubergine	*melitzana*/**μελιτζάνα (f.)**
beans french	*fasolakia prasina*/**φασολάκια πράσινα (n.)**
broad	*kookia*/**κουκιά (n.)**
cabbage	*lahano*/**λάχανο (n.)**
carrot	*karoto*/**καρότο (n.)**
courgettes	*kolokithakia*/**κολοκυθάκια (n.)**
cucumber	*angoori*/**αγγούρι (n.)**
garlic	*skortho*/**σκόρδο (n.)**
lettuce	*marooli*/**μαρούλι (n.)**
olives	*elies*/**ελιές (f.)**
onion	*kremithi*/**κρεμμύδι (n.)**

TOPIC VOCABULARY

pea	*bizeli*/**μπιζέλι** (n.)
pepper	*piperia*/**πιπεριά** (f.)
potato	*patata*/**πατάτα** (f.)
salad (peasant) salad	*salata horiatiki*/**σαλάτα χωριάτικη** (f.)
prawn salad	*garithosalata*/**γαριδοσαλάτα** (f.)
green salad	*prasini salata*/**πράσινη σαλάτα** (f.)
russian salad	*rossiki salata*/**ρωσσική σαλάτα** (f.)
tomato	*domata*/**ντομάτα** (f.)
vine leaves (stuffed)	*dolmathes*/**ντολμάδες** (m.)
yoghurt and garlic dip	*tzatziki*/**τζατζίκι** (n.)

Fish

cod	*bakaliaros*/**μπακαλιάρος** (m.)
crab	*kavoori*/**καβούρι** (n.)
crayfish	*karavitha*/**καραβίδα** (f.)
lobster	*astakos*/**αστακός** (m.)
mussels	*mithia*/**μύδια** (n.)
octopus	*htapothi*/**χταπόδι** (n.)
prawns	*garithes*/**γαρίδες** (f.)
red mullet	*barbooni*/**μπαρμπούνι** (n.)
sardine	*sarthela*/**σαρδέλλα** (f.)
shrimps	*garithes*/**γαρίδες** (f.)
squid	*kalamari*/**καλαμάρι** (n.)
(baby) squid	*kalamaraki*/**καλαμαράκι** (n.)
swordfish	*ksifias*/**ξιφίας** (m.)
tuna	*tonos*/**τόνος** (m.)

Meat

bacon	*beikon*/**μπέϊκον** (n.)
beef	*vothino*/**βοδινό** (n.)
chicken	*kotopoolo*/**κοτόπουλο** (n.)
chops	*brizoles*/**μπριζόλες** (f.)
ham	*jambon*/**ζαμπόν** (n.)
kebab	*soovlaki*/**σουβλάκι** (n.)
lamb	*arni*/**αρνί** (n.)
lamb chops	*paithakia*/**παϊδάκια** (n.)
meat balls	*keftethes*/**κεφτέδες** (m.)
pork	*hirino*/**χοιρινό** (n.)
sausage	*lookaniko*/**λουκάνικο** (n.)
steak	*brizola*/**μπριζόλα** (f.)
veal	*moshari*/**μοσχάρι** (n.)

Groceries

bread	*psomi*/**ψωμί** (n.)
biscuits	*biskota*/**μπισκότα** (n.)
butter	*vootiro*/**βούτυρο** (n.)
cake	*keik*/**κέϊκ** (n.)
cheese feta	*tiri feta*/**τυρί** (n.) **φέτα**
gouda	*tiri gooda*/**τυρί** (n.) **γκούντα**
cheese pie	*tiropita*/**τυρόπιττα** (f.)

TOPIC VOCABULARY

coffee	*kafes*/**καφές** (m.)
eggs	*avga*/**αυγά** (n.)
milk	*ghala*/**γάλα** (n.)
nuts (pistachio)	*fistikia*/**φυστίκια** (n.)
oil	*lathi*/**λάδι** (n.)
olive oil	*eleolatho*/**ελαιόλαδο** (n.)
pasta	*zimarika*/**ζυμαρικά** (n.)
pepper	*piperi*/**πιπέρι** (n.)
rice	*rizi*/**ρύζι** (n.)
salt	*alati*/**αλάτι** (n.)
spaghetti	*makaronia*/**μακαρόνια** (n.)
sugar	*zahari*/**ζάχαρη** (f.)
tea	*tsai*/**τσάϊ** (n.)
vinegar	*ksithi*/**ξύδι** (n.)
wine	*krasi*/**κρασί** (n.)
yoghurt	*yiaoorti*/**γιαούρτι** (n.)

Parts of the body

ankle	*astragalos*/**αστράγαλος** (m.)
arm	*bratso*/**μπράτσο** (n.)
back	*plati*/**πλάτη** (f.)
blood	*ema*/**αίμα** (n.)
bone	*kokalo*/**κόκκαλο** (n.)
breast	*stithos*/**στήθος** (n.)
chest	*stithos*/**στήθος** (n.)
ear	*afti*/**αυτί** (n.)
elbow	*angonas*/**αγκώνας** (m.)
eye	*mati*/**μάτι** (n.)
face	*prosopo*/**πρόσωπο** (n.)
finger	*thahtilo*/**δάχτυλο** (n.)
foot	*pothi*/**πόδι** (n.)
hair	*malia*/**μαλλιά** (n.)
hand	*heri*/**χέρι** (n.)
head	*kefali*/**κεφάλι** (n.)
heart	*kardia*/**καρδιά** (f.)
hip	*gofos*/**γοφός** (m.)
knee	*gonato*/**γόνατο** (n.)
leg	*pothi*/**πόδι** (n.)
lips	*hilia*/**χείλια** (n.)
lungs	*pnevmones*/**πνεύμονες** (m.)
mouth	*stoma*/**στόμα** (n.)
muscle	*mis*/**μυς** (m.)
neck	*lemos*/**λαιμός** (m.)
nose	*miti*/**μύτη** (f.)
rib	*plevro*/**πλευρό** (n.)
shoulder	*omos*/**ώμος** (m.)
skin	*therma*/**δέρμα** (n.)
stomach	*stomahi*/**στομάχι** (n.)
thigh	*miros*/**μηρός** (m.)
throat	*lemos*/**λαιμός** (m.)
thumb	*andihiras*/**αντίχειρας** (m.)

TOPIC VOCABULARY

tooth	*thondi*/**δόντι** (n.)
toe	*thahtilo*/**δάχτυλο** (n.)
tongue	*glossa*/**γλώσσα** (f.)
waist	*messi*/**μέση** (f.)
wrist	*karpos*/**καρπός** (m.)

Sports and games

ball	*bala*/**μπάλλα** (f.)
basketball	*basket*/**μπάσκετ** (n.)
beach	*paralia*/**παραλία** (f.)
boat	*varka*/**βάρκα** (f.)
canoe	*kano*/**κανώ** (n.)
canoing	*kano kano*/**κάνω κανώ**
cards	*trapooloharta*/**τραπουλόχαρτα** (n.)
cycling	*pothilatothromia*/**ποδηλατοδρομία** (f.)
dancing	*horos*/**χορός** (m.)
dinghy	*mikri varka*/**μικρή βάρκα** (f.)
fishing	*psarema*/**ψάρεμα** (n.)
floats (for kids' arms)	*bratsakia*/**μπρατσάκια** (n.)
football	*pothosfero*/**ποδόσφαιρο** (n.)
golf	*golf*/**γκόλφ** (n.)
jogging	*jogging*/**τζόγκινγκ** (n.)
pedal boat	*pothilato thalassas*/**ποδήλατο θάλασσας** (n.)
sailing	*istioploia*/**ιστιοπλοΐα** (f.)
skiing	*ski*/**σκί** (n.)
speedboat	*kris-kraft*/**κρις-κράφτ** (n.)
sunbathing	*iliotherapia*/**ηλιοθεραπεία** (f.)
swimming	*kolimbi*/**κολύμπι** (n.)
swimming pool	*pisina*/**πισίνα** (f.)
tennis	*tennis*/**τέννις** (n.)
tennis court	*yipetho tennis*/**γήπεδο τέννις** (n.)
tennis racket	*raketa tennis*/**ρακέτα τέννις** (f.)
volleyball	*vollei bol*/**βόλλεϋ-μπώλ** (n.)
walking	*perpatima*/**περπάτημα** (n.)
waterskiing	*thalassio ski*/**θαλάσσιο σκί** (n.)
windsurfing	*gooindserfing*/**γουϊντσέρφινγκ** (n.)

Leisure, entertainment, sightseeing

art gallery	*galleri*/**γκαλλερί** (f.)
bar	*bar*/**μπάρ** (n.)
bouzouki place	*kendro*/**κέντρο** (n.)
castle	*kastro*/**κάστρο** (n.)
cathedral	*kathethrikos naos*/**καθεδρικός ναός** (m.)
cave	*spilia*/**σπηλιά** (f.)
church	*eklisia*/**εκκλησία** (f.)
cinema	*kinimatografos*/**κινηματογράφος** (m.)
coast	*akti*/**ακτή** (f.)
disco	*diskotek*/**ντισκοτέκ** (f.)
excursion	*ekthromi*/**εκδρομή** (f.)
film	*tenia*/**ταινία** (f.)

TOPIC VOCABULARY

island	*nisi*/**νησί** (n.)
lake	*limni*/**λίμνη** (f.)
monastery	*monastiri*/**μοναστήρι** (n.)
monument	*mnimio*/**μνημείο** (n.)
mountain	*voono*/**βουνό** (n.)
museum	*moosio*/**μουσείο** (n.)
night club	*nihterino kendro*/**νυχτερινό κέντρο** (n.)
restaurant	*estiatorio*/**εστιατόριο** (n.)
ruin	*eripio*/**ερείπιο** (n.)
sea	*thalassa*/**θάλασσα** (f.)
taverna	*taverna*/**ταβέρνα** (f.)
view	*thea*/**θέα** (f.)
wall	*tihos*/**τείχος** (n.)

Weather

clear	*ethrios*/**αίθριος**
cloud	*sinnefo*/**σύννεφο** (n.)
cloudy	*sinnefiasmenos*/**συννεφιασμένος**
cold	*krio*/**κρύο** (n.)
cool	*throsia*/**δροσιά** (f.)
drizzle	*psihalisma*/**ψιχάλισμα** (n.)
hot	*zestos*/**ζεστός**
lightning	*astrapi*/**αστραπή** (f.)
rain	*vrohi*/**βροχή** (f.)
rainy	*vroheros*/**βροχερός**
shower	*boorini*/**μπουρίνι** (n.)
sky	*ooranos*/**ουρανός** (m.)
sun	*ilios*/**ήλιος** (m.)
sunny	*liakatha*/**λιακάδα** (f.)
thunder	*vrondi*/**βροντή** (f.)
umbrella	*ombrella*/**ομπρέλλα** (f.)
wind	*anemos*/**άνεμος** (m.)
windy	*anemothis*/**ανεμώδης**

Souvenirs

classical copy (of an ancient design/statue)	*andigrafo*/**αντίγραφο** (n.)
handbag	*tsanda*/**τσάντα** (f.)
hand-made	*hiropiitos/i/o*/**χειροποίητος-η-ο**
head (statue)	*kefali (agalmatos)*/**κεφαλή (αγάλματος)**
jewellery	*kosmimata*/**κοσμήματα** (n.)
leather	*therma*/**δέρμα** (n.)
leather goods	*thermatina ithi*/**δερμάτινα είδη** (n.)
necklace	*kolie*/**κολλιέ** (n.)
pottery	*keramiki*/**κεραμική** (f.)
statue	*agalma*/**άγαλμα** (n.)
vase	*vazo*/**βάζο** (n.)
weave	*ifando*/**υφαντό** (n.)
worry beads	*komboloi*/**κομπολόϊ** (n.)

VOCABULARY

GREEK–ENGLISH VOCABULARY

Άγαλμα *aghalma* (n.) statue
αγαπάω *aghapao* to love
Αγγλία *Anglia* (f.) England
Άγγλος *Anglos* (m.) English(man)
Αγγλίδα *Anglitha* (f.) English(woman)
αγγλικός *anglikos* (m.) English
  (adjective)
αγγλικά *anglika* (n.) English
  (language)
αγγούρι *angoori* (n.) cucumber
άγιος; αγία *ayios* (m.), *ayia* (f.) saint
αγορά *agora* (f.) market
αγοράζω *agorazo* to buy
άδεια οδηγήσεως *athia othigiseos* (f.)
  driving licence
αδελφή *athelfi* (f.) sister
αέρας *aeras* (m.) wind
ΑΔΙΕΞΟΔΟΣ *athieksothos* No
  through road
αεροδρόμιο, αερολιμένας *aerothromio,*
  aerolimenas (n.), (m) airport
αεροπλάνο *aeroplano* (n.) airplane
αεροπορικώς *aeroporikos* by air
αίθουσα αναμονής *ethoosa anamonis*
  waiting room
αισθάνομαι *esthanome* to feel
ακτοφύλακας *aktofilakas* (m.)
  lifeguard
ακτή *akti* (f.) coast
ακριβό *akrivo* expensive
αλάτι *alati* (n.) salt
(να) αλλάξει, (αλλάζω) *(na) alaksi,*
  (alazo) to change (I change)
αλλεργικός *alergikos* allergic
αλλεργικό συνάχι *allergiko sinahi* (n.)
  hay fever
αλήθεια *alithia* really, actually
αλοιφή *alifi (f.)* ointment
αμέσως *amesos* immediately
άμμος *amos* (f.) sand
αμφιθέατρο *amfitheatro* (n.)
  amphitheatre
αμφορέας *amforeas* (m.) amphora
αναπτήρας *anaptiras* (m.) lighter
ΑΝΑΧΩΡΗΣΕΙΣ *anahorisis*
  departures
αναψυκτικά *anapsiktika* (n.)
  refreshments
ΑΝΔΡΩΝ *anthron* gents (toilet)

άνθρωπος *anthropos* (m.) man
αντηλιακό (λάδι) *andiliako (lathi)* (n.)
  suntan oil
αντισυλληπτικά (χάπια) *andisiliptika*
  (hapia) (n.) contraceptive (pills)
αντίο *andio* goodbye
άντρας *andras* (m.) man
απόδειξη *apothiksi* (f.) receipt
ΑΝΟΙΚΤΟ *anikto* open
ΑΠΑΓΟΡΕΥΕΤΑΙ *apagorevete* it is
  forbidden
απέναντι *apenandi* opposite
απλώς *aplos* simply, just
απόγευμα *apoyevma* (n.) afternoon
αποσκευές *aposkeves* (f.) luggage
αρέσει (μ'αρέσει) *aressi (m'aressi)*
  I like (it)
μ'αρέσουν *m'aressoon* I like (them)
αριθμός *arithmos* (m.) number
αριστερά *aristera* left
αρνάκι *arnaki* (n.) lamb
αρνί *arni* (n.) mutton
άρρωστος *arostos* ill, sick
αρχαιολογικός τόπος *arheologikos*
  topos (m.) archaeological site
αρχαία *arhea* antiquities
αρχαία ελληνική τραγωδία *arhea*
  elliniki tragothia classical Greek
  tragedy
ασανσέρ *asanser* (n.) lift
ασθενοφόρο *asthenoforo* (n.)
  ambulance
άσπρο *aspro* white
ασπιρίνη *aspirini* (f.) aspirin
αστράγαλος *astragalos* (m.) ankle
αστυνομία *astinomia* (f.) police
αστυνομικό τμήμα *astinomiko tmima*
  (n.) police station
ασφάλεια *asfalia* (f.) insurance
άσχημος καιρός *ashimos keros* (m.)
  bad weather
άτομα *atoma* (n.) people
αυγό *avgo* (n.) egg
αύριο *avrio* tomorrow
αυτοκίνητο *aftokinito* (n.) car
αυτός *aftos* this
ΑΦΙΞΕΙΣ *Afiksis* Arrivals
Αχθοφόρε! *Ahthofore!* (m.) Porter!
αχλάδια *ahlathia* (n.) pears

VOCABULARY

Βαλίτσα valitsa (f.) suitcase
βάζο vazo (n.) vase
βάλτε (βάζω) valte (vazo) to put (I put)
βαμβακερό vamvakero cotton
βάρκα varka (f.) boat
βάρκα με μηχανή varka me mihani motor boat
βάρκα με πανί varka me pani sailing boat
βέβαια/βεβαίως vevea/veveos of course
βαθειά vathia deep
βαπόρι vapori (n.) ship
βενζίνη (απλή) venzini (apli) (f.) petrol (regular)
βερύκοκα verikoka (n.) apricots
βεράντα veranda (f.) verandah
βήχας vihas (m.) cough
βλάβη vlavi (f.) breakdown
βλέπω vlepo to see
βοήθεια! voithia! Help!
(να σας) βοηθήσει (βοηθάω) (na sas) voithisi (voithao) to help you (I help)
βουνό voono (n.) mountain
βούτυρο vootiro (n.) butter
βράδι vrathi (n.) evening
βραδινό vrathino (n.) supper
βραστό vrasto boiled
βρέχει vrehi it is raining
βροχή vrohi (f.) rain

Γάλα ghala (n.) milk
γαρίδα gharitha (f.) shrimp
γεμάτοι yemati full
γεμίστε (γεμίζω) yemiste (yemizo) fill (I fill)
γεύμα yevma (n.) meal
Γειά σου yia soo hello/goodbye (informal)
γερανός yeranos (m.) crane
γιαούρτι yiaoorti (n.) yoghurt
για yia for
για μια νύχτα yia mia nihta for one night
γιατρός yiatros (m.) doctor
γκαράζ garaz (n.) garage
γίνομαι yinome to become
γκαρσόν garson (n.) waiter
γκισέ gisé (n.) cash desk
γκρί gri grey
γλυκά glika (n.) sweets, desserts
γράμμα grama (n.) letter

γραμματόσημα gramatosima (n.) stamps
γραμματοκιβώτιο gramatokivotio (n.) mailbox
Γραφείο Τουρισμού Grafio Toorismoo (n.) Tourist Office
γρήγορα grigora quickly
γυαλιά ηλίου yialia ilioo (n.) sunglasses
γυναίκα yineka (f.) woman
ΓΥΝΑΙΚΩΝ Yikenon ladies (toilet)
γύρος yiros (m.) tour
γωνία gonia (f.) corner

Δείπνο thipno (n.) dinner
δέκα theka ten
δεξιά theksia on the right
δεσποινίς thespinis (f.) miss
Δευτέρα theftera (f.) Monday
διερμηνέας thiermineas (m.) interpreter
διαβατήριο thiavatirio (n.) passport
(να μου) δείξετε (δείχνω) (na moo) thiksete (thihno) to show me (I show)
δείξτε (μου) (δείχνω) thikste (moo) (thihno) show (me) (I show)
δελτίο καιρού theltio keroo (n.) weather forecast
διάλειμμα thialima (n.) interval
διαμέρισμα thiamerisma (n.) flat
Διανυκτερεύον thianikterevon open all night
διακόσια thiakosia two hundred
διακοπές thiakopes (f.) holidays
διάρροια thiaria (f.) diarrhoea
διασκεδάζω thiaskethazo to enjoy myself
διασταύρωση thiastavrosi (f.) crossroads
διεύθυνση thiefthinsi (f.) address
δίκλινο thiklino (n.) double room
(Μας δίνετε) δίνω (Mas thinete) thino (thino) Would you give us (I give)
δικηγόρος thikigoros (m.) lawyer
δίκιο thikio (n.) right
διόδια thiothia (n.) toll
διψάω thipsao to be thirsty
δοκιμαστήρια thokimastiria (n.) changing rooms
δοκιμάστε (τα) (δοκιμάζω) thokimaste (ta) (thokimazo) try (them) on, (I try on)
δολλάρια tholaria (n.) dollars

VOCABULARY

δράμα *thrama* (n.) drama
δραχμή *thrahmi* (f.) drachma
δουλειά *thoolia* (f.) job
ΔΡΟΜΟΛΟΓΙΑ *thromologia* (n.)
  timetables
δρόμος *thromos* (m.) road, street
δύο *thio* two
δροσιά *throsia* (f.) cool (weather)
δύσκολα *thiskola* difficult
δυστύχημα *thistihima* (n.) accident
δυστυχώς *thistihos* unfortunately
δώδεκα *thotheka* twelve
δωμάτιο *thomatio* (n.) room
δώστε (μου), (δίνω) *thoste* (*moo*),
  (*thino*) give (me), (I give)

Εβδομάδα *evthomatha* (f.) week
εβδομαδιαίος, α, ο *evthomathieos*
  weekly
έγκαυμα *engavma* (n.) burn
έγκυος *engyos* (f.) pregnant
εγώ *ego* I
έγχρωμο φίλμ *enhromo film* (n.)
  colour film
εδώ *etho* here
εθνική οδός *ethniki othos* (f.) main
  street
είκοσι *ikosi* twenty
είμαι *ime* I am
είμαστε *imaste* we are
εισιτήριο *isitirio* (n.) ticket
εισιτήριο με επιστροφή *isitirio me*
  epistrofi (n.) return ticket
είσοδος *isothos* (f.) entrance
εκατό *ekato* a hundred
εκδρομή *ekthromi* (f.) excursion
εκεί *eki* there
έκθεση *ekthesi* (f.) exhibition
εκεί πέρα *eki pera* over there
εκκλησία *eklisia* (f.) church
εκείνος, η, ο *ekinos* that
εκπτώσεις *ekptosis* (f.) sales
έκοψα, (κόβω) *ekopsa*, (*kovo*) I've
  cut, (I cut)
έκαψα, (καίω) *ekapsa*, (*keo*) I've
  burnt, (I burn)
έκλεψαν, (κλέβω) *eklepsan*, (*klevo*)
  they stole, (I steal)
ελάτε, (έρχομαι) *elate*, (*erhome*)
  come, (I come)
Έλεγχος διαβατηρίων *elenhos*
  thiavatirion (m.) Passport Control
ελιές *elies* (f.) olives
Ελλάδα *Ellatha* (f.) Greece

Έλληνας *Ellinas* (m.) Greek (man)
Ελληνίδα *Ellinitha* (f.) Greek
  (woman)
Ελληνικός, η, ο *Ellinikos* Greek
  (adjective)
Ελληνικά *Ellinika* (n.) Greek
  (language)
ένα *ena* one
ένας, μία, ένα *enas, mia, ena* a, an
ένδεκα *entheka* eleven
ενενήντα *eneninda* ninety
εννιά *ennia* nine
εννιακόσια *enniakosia* nine hundred
ενοικιάσεις αυτοκινήτων *enikiasis*
  aftokiniton car rental
εντάξει *entaksi* it's all right
εξακόσια *Eksakosia* six hundred
εξήντα *Eksinda* sixty
έξι *Eksi* six
έξοδος *Eksothos* (f.) exit
ΕΞΟΔΟΣ ΚΙΝΔΥΝΟΥ *Eksothos*
  kinthinoo emergency exit
εξώστης *Eksostis* (m.) upper circle
επιταγή *epitayi* (f.) order, cheque
επιπλέον *epipleon* moreover
επιδόρπιο *epithorpio* (n.) dessert
επίδεσμος *epithesmos* (m.) bandage
να επιδιορθώσετε (επιδιορθώνω) *na*
  epithiorthosete (*epithiorthono*)
  to repair (I repair)
έπεσα, (πέφτω) *epesa*, (*pefto*) I've
  fallen (I fall)
επικίνδυνος, η, ο *epikinthinos, i, o*
  dangerous
επόμενος, η, ο *epomenos, i, o* next
έπαθα (παθαίνω) *epatha* (*patheno*)
  I've suffered (I suffer)
επείγον *epigon* urgent
έπιασε φωτιά *epiase fotia* it's caught
  fire
επίσκεψη *episkepsi* (f.) visit
να έρθει (έρχομαι) *na erthi* (*erhome*)
  to come (I come)
(σας) έρχεται καλά (*sas*) *erhete kala* it
  fits you well
έσκασε το λάστιχο *eskase to lastiho*
  I've had a puncture
ερείπια *eripia* (n.) ruins
εσείς *esis* you (formal)
εσπρέσσο *espresso* (m.) espress
εστιατόριο *estiatorio* (n.) restaur
έτοιμο *etimo* ready
ευθεία *efthia* (f.) straight ahead
ευχαριστώ *efharisto* thank you

VOCABULARY

εφτά *efta* seven
εφτακόσια *eftakosia* seven hundred
έχετε καθόλου... *ehete katholoo...*
  have you got any ...
έχω κλείσει *eho klisi* I've booked
έχασα (χάνω) *ehasa (hano)* I've lost
  (I lose)
εσύ *esi* you (informal)
εφημερίδα *efimeritha* (f.) newspaper
εύκολος, η, ο *efkolos, i, o* easy

Ζακέττα *zaketta* (f.) jacket
ζάχαρη *zahari* (f.) sugar
Ζαχαροπλαστείο *Zaharoplastio* (n.)
  pastry shop
ζέστη *zesti* (f.) heat
ζεστός, η, ο *zestos, i, o* hot
ζευγάρι *zevgari* (n.) pair
ζώνη *zoni* (f.) belt

Ἡλιος *ilios* (m.) sun
ηλίαση *iliasi* (f.) sunstroke
ημερήσιος, α, ο *imerisios, a, o* daily
ημερομηνία *imerominia* (f.) date
ήρεμος, η, ο *iremos, i, o* calm (the
  sea)
ήμουνα (είμαι) *imoona (ime)* I was
  (I am)
ήσυχος, η, ο *isihos, i, o* quiet
ήπιαμε, (πίνω) *ipiame, (pino)* we
  drank, (I drink)

Θάλασσα *thalassa* (f.) sea
θαλασσινά *thalassina* (n.) seafood
θαλάσσιο σκι *thalassio ski* (n.) water-
  skiing
θαυμάσιος, α, ο *thavmasios, a, o*
  wonderful
θέα *thea* (f.) view
θέατρο *theatro* (n.) theatre
θέλω... *thelo* I want/I'd like
θέλετε... *thelete* Do you want/would
  you like
θερμοκρασία *thermokrasia* (f.)
  temperature
θέση *thesi* (f.) seat
θυμάμαι *thimame* I remember

Καθαρός, η, ο *katharos* clean, clear
καθένας *kathenas* everyone
κάθε *kathe* each
καθίστε (κάθομαι) *kathiste* sit (I sit)
καθρέφτης *kathreftis* (m.) mirror
καθυστέρηση *kathisterisi* (f.) delay

καιρός *keros* (m.) weather
(Πόσο) καιρό... *(Poso) kero...?* How
  long ...?
καλά *kala* well
καλαμαράκια *kalamarakia* (n.) squids
καλημέρα *kalimera* good morning
καληνύχτα *kalinihta* good night
καλησπέρα *kalispera* good evening
καλός καιρός *kalos keros* good
  weather
καλσόν *kalson* (n.) tights
κάλτσες *kaltses* (f.) socks, stockings
κάμπινγκ *kamping* (n.) campsite
καμπίνα *kambina* (f.) cubicle
κάνει ζέστη *kani zesti* it's hot
κανώ *kano* (n.) canoe
καλώς ωρίσατε! *kalos orisate*
  welcome!
καπέλλο *kapelo* (n.) hat
καπνίζω *kapnizo* to smoke
καπουτσίνο *kapootsino* (m.)
  cappuccino
καράβι *karavi* (n.) boat
καραμέλλες *karamelles* (f.) sweets
καρδιακός, η, ο *karthiakos* person
  suffering from his heart
καρέκλα *karekla* (f.) chair
καρότα *karota* (n.) carrots
καρπούζι *karpoozi* (n.) watermelon
κάρτα *karta* (f.) card
καρχαρίας *karharias* (m.) shark
κασσετόφωνο *kassetophono* (n.) tape-
  recorder
καταλαβαίνω *katalaveno* to
  understand
κατάλογος *katalogos* (m.) menu
κατάστημα *katastima* (n.) store
κατάστρωμα *katastroma* (n.) deck
καφέ *kafe* brown
καφενείο *kafenio* (n.) café
καφές *kafes* (m.) coffee
κέικ *keik* (n.) cake
κέντρο *kendro* (n.) town
  centre/bouzouki place
κεράσια *kerasia* (n.) cherries
κεφτέδες *keftethes* (m.) meatballs
κιθάρα *kithara* (f.) guitar
κι εσείς *ki esis* and you (formal)
κι εσύ *ki esi* and you (informal)
κιλό *kilo* (n.) kilo
κίνδυνος *kinthinos* (m.) danger
κινηματογράφος *kinimatografos* (m.)
  cinema
κίτρινο *kitrino* yellow

VOCABULARY

κλειδί *klithi* (n.) key
κλειστός, η, ο *klistos* closed
κλείνω εισιτήρια *klino isitiria* to book tickets
κοιτάω *kitao* to look at
κλοπή *klopi* (f.) theft
κόκα-κόλα *koka-kola* (f.) coke
κόκκινο *kokino* red
κολοκυθάκια *kolokithakia* (n.) courgettes
κόλπος *kolpos* (m.) gulf
κολύμπι *kolimbi* (n.) swimming
κολυμπώ *kolimbo* to swim
κολώνα *kolona* (f.) column
κονιάκ *koniak* (n.) brandy
κονσέρβα *konserva* (f.) tin
κομμάτι *kommati* (n.) piece of
κοντός, η, ο *kondos* short
κοστίζει *kostizi* it costs
κοτόπουλο *kotopoolo* (n.) chicken
κουτάλι *kootali* (n.) spoon
κρασί γλυκό *krasi gliko* (n.) sweet wine
κρασί κόκκινο *krasi kokino* (n.) red wine
κρασί άσπρο *krasi aspro* (n.) white wine
κρασί ξηρό *krasi ksiro* (n.) dry wine
κρέας *kreas* (n.) meat
κρεβάτι *krevati* (n.) bed
κρέμα ηλίου *krema ilioo* (f.) suntan cream
κρεοπωλείο *kreopolio* (n.) butcher's shop
κρύο *krio* cold
κτίριο *ktirio* (n.) building
κυματώδης *kimatothis* very rough (sea)
κυκλοφορία *kikloforia* (f.) traffic
κυρία *kiria* (f.) Mrs.
Κυριακή *kiriaki* (f.) Sunday
κύριος *kirios* (m.) Mr.
κωμωδία *komothia* (f.) comedy

Λάδι *lathi* (n.) oil
λάδι ηλίου *lathi ilioo* (n.) suntan oil
λαϊκός χορός *laikos horos* (m.) folk dancing
λάθος *lathos* (n.) mistake
λαχανικά *lahanika* (n.) vegetables
λεμονάδα *lemonatha* (f.) lemonade
λεμόνι *lemoni* (n.) lemon
λέξη *leksi* (f.) word
λεπτό *lepto* (n.) minute

λεφτά *lefta* (n.) money
λεωφορείο *leoforio* (n.) bus
λεωφόρος *leoforos* (f.) avenue
λιακάδα *liakatha* (f.) sunshine
λίρα *lira* (f.) English pound
λίγο *ligo* a little
λικέρ *liker* (n.) liqueur
λιμάνι *limani* (n.) harbour
λίτρο *litro* (n.) litre
λογαριασμός *logariasmos* (m.) bill
λουκάνικα *lookanika* (n.) sausages
λουτρά *lootra* (n.) baths
λύκος *likos* (m.) wolf
λυπάμαι *lipame* I'm sorry

Μαγιό *mayio* (n.) bathing suit/trunks
(να) μάθω (μαθαίνω) *na matho* (*matheno*) to learn (I learn)
μακριά *makria* far
μακώ (μπλούζα) *mako* (*blooza*) (f.) tee-shirt
μάλιστα *malista* yes, of course
μάρκα *marka* (f.) make
μαρμελάδα *marmelatha* (f.) marmalade
μαρούλι *marooli* (n.) lettuce
μαύρο *mavro* black
μαχαίρι *maheri* (n.) knife
μαζί μας *mazi mas* with us
Μαντείο *mandio* (n.) Oracle
μέγεθος *meyethos* (n.) size
μεζέδες *mezethes* (m.) starters
μελιτζάνα *melitzana* (f.) aubergine
μενού *menoo* (n.) menu
μένω *meno* to live, to stay
μέρος *meros* (n.) part
μέχρι *mehri* till, to
με συγχωρείτε... *me sinhorite*... Excuse me...
μέρα *mera* (n.) day
μεσημέρι *mesimeri* (n.) noon
μεσημεριανό *mesimeriano* (n.) lunch
μετά *meta* after
μεταλλικό νερό *metalliko nero* (n.) mineral water
μέτρα *metra* (n.) metres
μέτριο *metrio* medium
μηδέν *mithen* zero
Μη καπνίζετε *Mi kapnizete* No Smoking
μήλο *milo* (n.) apple
μήνας *minas* (m.) month
μηχανή *mihani* (f.) engine
μηχανικός *mihanikos* (m.) mechanic

VOCABULARY

μητέρα *mitera* (f.) mother
μία *mia* a, an, one
μιλάω *milao* to speak
μιλάτε... *milate* Do you speak...?
μονόκλινο.... *monoklino*... single room
μονόδρομος *monothromos* (m.) one-way traffic
μοσχάρι *moshari* (n.) beef
μοσχαράκι *mosharaki* (n.) veal
μουσακάς *moosakas* (m.) moussaka
μουσικοχορευτικό *moosikohoreftiko* musical
μόνο *mono* only
μόνος *monos* alone
μουσείο *moosio* (n.) museum
μπακλαβάς *baklavas* (m.) baklava
μπάμιες *bamies* (f.) okra
μπάνιο *banio* (n.) bath
μπαρ *bar* (n.) bar
μπαρμπούνι *barbooni* (n.) red mullet
μπαταρία *bataria* (f.) battery
μπιζέλια *bizelia* (n.) peas
μπικίνι *bikini* (n.) bikini
μπισκότα *biskota* (n.) biscuits
μπλε *ble* blue
μπλούζα *blooza* (f.) blouse
Μπορώ να... *boro na*... May I...
μπριζόλες *brizoles* (f.) chops
μπουζούκι *boozooki* (n.) bouzouki
μπουκάλι *bookali* (n.) bottle
μπύρα *bira* (f.) beer

Ναι *ne* yes
ναός *naos* (m.) temple
ναυαγοσώστης *navagosostis* (m.) lifeguard
ναυτία *naftia* (f.) sea sickness
νέα *nea* (n.) news
νερό *nero* (n.) water
νησί *nisi* (n.) island
νοσοκομείο *nosokomio* (n.) hospital
νοικιάζω *nikiazo* to rent, to hire
νομίζω *nomizo* to think
νόμισμα *nomisma* (n.) coin
ντήζελ *diezel* diesel
ντισκοτέκ *diskotek* (f.) discotheque
ντολμάδες *dolmathes* (m.) stuffed vine leaves
ντομάτα *domata* (f.) tomato
ντομάτες γεμιστές *domates yemistes* stuffed tomatoes
ντοματόσουπα *domatosoopa* (f.) tomato soup

ντοματοσαλάτα *domatosalata* (f.) tomato salad
ντους *doosh* (n.) shower
νύχτα *nihta* (f.) night
νυχτερινό κέντρο *nihterino kendro* (n.) night club

Ξανά *ksana* again
ξαφνικά *ksafnika* suddenly
ξεκινάω *ksekinao* to start off
ξεναγός *ksenagos* (m., f.) guide
Ξενοδοχείο *ksenothohio* (n.) hotel
ξέρω *ksero* to know
ξυριστική μηχανή *ksiristiki mihani* (f.) electric razor
ξιφίας *ksifias* (m.) swordfish

Ογδόντα *ogthonda* eighty
οδηγός *othigos* (m.) guide book, driver
οδηγείτε (οδηγώ) *othigite* (*othigo*) to drive (I drive)
οδική κυκλοφορία *othiki kikloforia* (f.) traffic
οδικός χάρτης *othikos hartis* (m.) road map
οδοντόβουρτσα *othondovoortsa* (f.) toothbrush
οδοντογιατρός *othondoyiatros* (m.) dentist
οδοντόκρεμα *othondokrema* (f.) toothpaste
οδός *othos* (f.) street
ομελέττα *omeletta* (f.) omelette
οικογένεια *ikoyenia* (f.) family
ομπρέλλα ηλίου *ombrella ilioo* (f.) beach umbrella
όνομα *onoma* (n.) name
ορεκτικά *orektika* (n.) starters
ορίστε *oriste* here you are
όριο ταχύτητας *orio tahititas* (n.) speed limit
όροφος *orofos* (m.) floor
ούζο *oozo* (n.) ouzo
όχι *ohi* no
οκτακόσια *oktakosia* eight hundred
οκτώ *okto* eight

Παγωμένος, η, ο *pagomenos* iced, chilled
παϊδάκια *paithakia* (n.) lamb chops
πάγκος *pagos* (m.) bench
παγωτό *pagoto* (n.) ice-cream
παθαίνω *patheno* to suffer

VOCABULARY

παίρνω *perno* to take
πακέτο τσιγάρα *paketo tsigara* (n.)
  packet of cigarettes
παιδί *pethi* (n.) child
παιχνίδι *pehnithi* (n.) toy, game
παντελόνι *pandeloni* (n.) trousers
παντρεμένος, η *pandremenos* married
παντού *pandoo* everywhere
παράδοση *parathosi* (f.) tradition
παρακαλώ *parakalo* please, don't
  mention it
παράκαμψη *parakampsi* (f.) detour
παραλία *paralia* (f.) beach
πάρκινγκ *parking* (n.) parking
Παρασκευή *Paraskevi* (f.) Friday
παράσταση *parastasi* (f.) performance
πάρτε (παίρνω) *parte* (*perno*) to take
  (I take)
παρκόμετρο *parkometro* (n.) parking
  meter
πατάτες *patates* (f.) potatoes
πατάτες τηγανητές *patates tiganites* (f.)
  chips
πεζόδρομος *pezothromos* (m.)
  pedestrian zone
Πέμπτη *Pempti* (f.) Thursday
πενήντα *peninda* fifty
πεντακόσια *pendakosia* five hundred
πέντε *pende* five
πεπόνι *peponi* (n.) melon
περιμένω *perimeno* to wait for
περιοδεία *periothia* (f.) tour
περιοδικό *periothiko* (n.) magazine
περίπου *peripoo* about
περίπτερο *periptero* (n.) kiosk
περνάω ωραία *pernao orea* to have a
  good time
πέτρες *petres* (f.) stones
πετσέτα *petseta* (f.) towel
πηγαίνω *piyeno* to go
πηρούνι *pirooni* (n.) fork
πιάτο *piato* (n.) plate
πίεση *piesi* (f.) blood-pressure
(να) πιούμε (πίνω) *na pioome* (*pino*)
  to drink (I drink)
πιπέρι *piperi* (n.) pepper
πιπεριές *piperies* (f.) peppers
πισίνα *pisina* (f.) swimming pool
πιστωτική κάρτα *pistotiki karta* (f.)
  credit card
πλαζ *plaj* (f.) beach
πλατεία *platia* (f.) square, stalls
πληροφορίες *plirofories* (f.)
  information

πλάτη *plati* (f.) back (anat.)
πλησιέστερος, η, ο *plisiesteros, i, o*
  nearest
να πληρώσετε (πληρώνω) *na plirosete*
  (*plirono*) to pay (I pay)
(με τα) πόδια (*me ta*) *pothia* on foot
ποδήλατο θάλασσας *pothilato thalassas*
  (n.) pedal boat
ποιός-α-ο; *pios, a, o?* who?
πλήρης ασφάλεια *pliris asfalia* full
  insurance
πλοίο *plio* (n.) ship
πνίγεται *pniyetai* he/she is drowning
πόλη *poli* (f.) city
πολύ *poli* very much
πολυθρόνα *polithrona* (f.) armchair
(με) πονάει (*me*) *ponai* it hurts
πόνος *ponos* (m) pain
πονόδοντος *ponothondos* (m.)
  toothache
πονοκέφαλος *ponokefalos* (m.) headache
πόρτα *porta* (f.) door
πορτοκαλάδα *portokalatha* (f.)
  orangeade
πορτοκάλι *portokali* (n.) orange
πορτ-μπαγκάς *port-bagaz (n.) boot (of*
  car)
πρατήριο βενζίνης *pratirio venzinis*
  (n.) petrol station
πόσιμο *posimo* drinkable
πόσο...; *poso?* How much...?
πότε...; *pote?* when...?
πόσα...; *posa?* How many...?
ποτήρι *potiri* (n.) glass
ποτό *poto* (n.) drink
πουλόβερ *poolover* (n.)
  sweater/pullover
πουκάμισο *pookamiso* (n.) shirt
πούρο *pooro* (n.) cigar
πούλμαν *poolman* (n.) coach
πράσινο *prasino* green
προβλήματα *provlimata* (n.) problems
πρεσβεία *presvia* (f.) embassy
πρησμένος *prismenos* swollen
πρόγραμμα *programma* (n.)
  programme
προκαταβολή *prokatavoli* (f.) deposit
προορισμός *proorismos* (m.)
  destination
προσοχή *prosohi* caution, attention
πρόσκληση *prosklisi* (f.) invitation
πρωί *proi* (n.) morning
πρωινό *proino* (n.) breakfast
πτήση *ptisi* (f.) flight

VOCABULARY

πυρετός *piretos* (m.) fever
πυροσβέστης *pirosvestis* (m.) fireman
πυροσβεστική αντλία *pirosvestiki andlia* (f.) fire brigade

Ρέστα *resta* change
ρετσίνα *retsina* (f.) retsina
ροδάκινα *rothakina* (n.) peaches
ρολόϊ *roloi* (n.) clock, watch
ρύζι *rizi* (n.) rice

Σάββατο *Savato* (n.) Saturday
Σαββατοκύριακο *savatokyriako* (n.) week-end
σάλτσα *saltsa* (f.) sauce
σαμπουάν *sampooan* (n.) shampoo
σάντουιτς *sandooits* (n.) sandwich
σαπούνι *sampooni* (n.) soap
σαράντα *saranda* forty
σειρά *sira* turn
σερβιέττες υγείας *serviettes ighias* (f.) sanitary towels
σημαδούρα *simathoora* (f.) buoy
σήμερα *simera* today
(πιο) σιγά *(pio) siga* more slowly
σίγουρος, η, ο *sigooros, i, o* certain
σιδηρόδρομος *sithirothromos* (m.) railway
σινεμά *sinema* (n.) cinema
σκέτος καφές *sketos kafes* coffee without sugar
σλάϊντς *slaids* (n.) slides
σόδα *sotha* (f.) soda
σοκολάτα *sokolata* (f.) chocolate
σουβλάκι *soovlaki* (n.) souvlaki
σούπα *soopa* (f.) soup
σούπερ βενζίνη *sooper venzini* (f.) super petrol
σπασμένος *spasmenos* broken
σπουδάζω *spoothazo* to study
σπρέϊ *sprei* (n.) spray
σπίτι *spiti* (n.) house
στάδιο *stathio* (n.) stadium
σταθμός *stathmos* (m.) station
σταμάτησε (σταματάω) *stamatise (stamatao)* stop (I stop)
Σταθμός ταξί *stathmos taxi* taxi stand
Στάση *stasi* (f.) (bus) stop
σταφύλια *stafilia* (n.) grapes
στενό *steno* (n.) side street
στενός, η, ο *stenos* tight, narrow
στιγμή *stigmi* (f.) moment
στην υγειά σας! *stin ighia sas* cheers!
στραμπούληξα (στραμπουλίζω)

stramboliska (*stramboolizo*) I sprained (I sprain)
στρίψτε (στρίβω) *stripste (strivo)* turn (I turn)
στρώμα θάλασσας *stroma thalassas* airbed
στυλό *stilo* (n.) ballpoint pen
σύγκρουση *singroosi* (f.) collision
συγνώμη *signomi* sorry
σύκα *sika* (n.) figs
συμπληρώστε (συμπληρώνω) *simbliroste (simblirono)* fill in (I fill in)
συνάλλαγμα *sinallagma* (n.) currency exchange
συναυλία *sinavlia* (f.) concert
συνοδός *sinothos* (m.) guide
συννεφιά *sinnefia* (f.) cloudy
συνταγή *sindayi* (f.) prescription
συστημένο *sistimeno* register letter
συχνά *sihna* often
(να σας) συστηθώ *(na sas) sistitho* Let me introduce myself to you

Ταβέρνα *taverna* (f.) taverna
ταμείο *tamio* (n.) cash desk
ταξίδι *taksithi* (n.) trip
ταραμοσαλάτα *taramosalata* (f.) fish roe salad
ταχυδρομείο *tahithromio* (n.) Post Office
ταχύτητα *tahitita* (f.) speed
τελειώνω *teliono* to finish
τελωνείο *telonio* (n.) Customs
τέντα *tenda* (f.) tent
τηλεγράφημα *tilegrafima* (n.) telegram
τηλέφωνο *tilefono* (n.) telephone
τηλεφωνείστε (τηλεφωνώ) *tilefoniste (tilefono)* to telephone (I telephone)
τιμή *timi* (f.) price
τόστ *tost* (n.) toast
τουαλέττα *tooaletta* (f.) toilet
τσιγάρο *tsigaro* (n.) cigarette
τουρίστας *tooristas* (m.) tourist (man)
τουρίστρια *tooristria* (f.) tourist (woman)
Τουριστικός οδηγός *tooristikos othigos* (m.) tourist guide
Τουριστική Αστυνομία *touristiki astinomia* (f.) tourist police
τράπεζα *trapeza* (f.) bank
τροχόσπιτο *trohospito* (n.) trailer

VOCABULARY

τσάϊ με γάλα *tsai me gala* (n.) tea with milk

τσάϊ με λεμόνι *tsai me lemoni* (n.) tea with lemon

τυρί *tyri* (n.) cheese

τυρόπιττα *tyropitta* (f.) cheese pie

Υπάρχει *iparhi* there is

Υπογράψτε (υπογράφω) *ipograpste* (*ipografo*) to sign (I sign)

υπογραφή *ipografi* (f.) signature

ύφασμα *ifasma* (n.) material, fabric

υπόσχεσαι; (υπόσχομαι) *iposhese* (*iposhome*) do you promise? (I promise)

Φαγητό/φαΐ *fagito* (n.)/*fai* food

φάγαμε (τρώω) *fagame* (*tro-o*) we ate (I eat)

φάκελλος *fakellos* (m.) envelope

φανάρι *fanari* (n.) traffic lights

φαρμακείο *farmakio* (n.) chemist's shop

φασολάκια φρέσκα *fasolakia freska* (n.) green beans

φεριμπότ *feribot* (n.) ferry boat

φέτα *feta* (f.) feta cheese

φέρνω *ferno* I bring

φέτος *fetos* this year

φεύγω *fevgo* I leave

φιλοξενία *filoksenia* (f.) hospitality

φίλος, φίλη *filos* (m.), *fili* (f.) friend

φημισμένος, η, ο *fimismenos* famous

φοιτητής *fititis* (m.) student (male)

φοιτήτρια *fititria* (f.) student (female)

φόρεμα *forema* (n.) dress

φόρος *foros* (m.) tax

φράουλες *fraooles* (f.) strawberries

φραντζόλα *frantzola* (f.) loaf of bread

φρέσκος *freskos* fresh

φρούτα *froota* (n.) fruit

φτηνός, η, ο *ftinos* cheap

φτάνω *ftano* I arrive

φωτιά *fotia* (f.) fire

Χαίρετε *herete* hello/goodbye (formal)

χαίρομαι *herome* I'm glad

χάρηκα *harika* Pleased to have met you

χαίρω πολύ *hero poli* Pleased to meet you

χάρτης *hartis* (m.) map

χθες *hthes* yesterday

χαρτί τουαλέττας *harti tooalettas* toilet paper

χαρτονόμισμα *hartonomisma* (m.) note (money)

να χαλάσω (χαλάω) *na halaso* (*halao*) to change (I change) money

χάθηκε (χάνομαι) *hathike* (*hanome*) it got lost (I get lost)

χρέωση *hreosi* (f.) charge

χορός *horos* (m.) dance

χρειάζομαι *hriazome* I need

να χρησιμοποιήσω *ha hrisimopiiso* to use

χωριάτικη *horiatiki* traditional Greek salad

χωρίς *horis* without

Ψάρι *psari* (n.) fish

ψιλά *psila* (n.) change

ψωμί *psomi* (n.) bread

Ωραίος, α, ο *oreos, a, o* nice

ώρα *ora* time (f.) hour